# Gotcha!
### welcoming your adopted child home
A GUIDE FOR NEWLY ADOPTIVE PARENTS

*by*
*Patti M. Zordich, Ph.D.*

Copyright © 2011 by Patti M. Zordich, Ph.D.

All rights reserved. No portion of this book may be reproduced, stored in a retrieval system, or transmitted in any form or by any means – electronic, mechanical, photocopying, recording, or otherwise – without the written permission of the publisher:

All situations and characters appearing in this work are fictitious. Any resemblance to real incidents or persons, living or dead, is purely coincidental.

Published by CRICKENTREE PRESS®
1125 Kildaire Farm Rd., Suite 202, Cary, NC 27511
www.NewAdoptionResources.com
Email Info@NewAdoptionResources.com

Design and Illustration by Kevin Wynns
Stock photography from iStock and Restored Traditions

Printed in the United States of America

*To Tony R. Zordich,
my secure base.*


*To David Anthony Zordich,
my gift.*


*To Our Lady of Perpetual Help,
my mother and my hope.*

# Contents

Acknowledgements .............................................vii
Preface ................................................... ix
1  Dreams of Adoptive Parents ............................... 1
2  The "Mission" of Adopting an Orphaned Child ........... 4
3  The First Missing Piece: Nurturing ...................... 11
4  The Second Missing Piece: Early Relational Trauma ...... 18
5  The Third Missing Piece: Parenting is Hard! ............. 27
6  The Fourth Missing Piece: You .......................... 34
7  The Fifth Missing Piece: God .......................... 36
8  Cocooning™ Part I: What & Why? ...................... 39
9  Cocooning™ Part II: How? ............................. 45
10 Scheduling Activities Outside of Your Home ............ 59
11 Using Your Gotcha! Kit™................................66
Notes ................................................... 76
About the Author ....................................... 81

# Acknowledgements

Thank you to Joan Vondra, Ph.D. who gave me the incredible opportunity to learn so much about attachment. I couldn't have done this without Tony's love, support and encouragement. A huge hug to David, who challenged me to begin writing this book. Thank you to all of my child and parent clients who entrusted me to guide them on their healing journey, without whom this book would not have been possible. Thank you to Beverly Pajerski, Diana Romero, and Tony Zordich for giving their valuable time and suggestions in reading these pages and offering feedback. Lastly, thank you to my two mothers: Jean, who made it possible for me to have a passion for healing children with attachment trauma and for helping our family know how to be a family, and Our Lady of Perpetual Help who guides me to be a good mother to my son and my clients.

# Preface

This book is meant to provide you, the newly adoptive parent, with the necessary tools to love and emotionally nurture your newly adopted child. Teresa, The Little Flower said, "Trust and only trust should lead to love." [1] Building this trust is the journey for all parents and their child, but with adopted children, this journey is particularly challenging. Ideally, this book and The Gotcha! Kit has found its way into your life before bringing your little treasure home; however, it will help you no matter how long your child has been a part of your family.

Within these pages is a simple guide to create a loving, nurturing environment that will best facilitate a loving, secure bond between you and your newly adopted child. I call the process of creating this environment "Cocooning.™" Cocooning not only helps develop a positive attachment relationship between parent and child, it also helps to fill in the developmental needs your child missed in her first one to two years of life. This facilitates the crucial role of helping your child "to grow up on the inside." Through Cocooning, you make it possible for your child to begin maturing emotionally and developmentally.

The key to Cocooning effectively is simple. Simple, but not easy. The key is to strive to see your child through God's eyes. Who is this child whom God has created? We can know, as King David did in Psalm 139:14, "... I am wondrously made. Wonderful are your works! You know me right well."[2] The key to Cocooning is to discover this wonderful being God knit in her mother's womb. As David cried out, "Search me, O God, and know my heart![3]" Cocooning will make it possible for you to search your child and to know her heart.

> *I praise you, for I am wondrously made. Wonderful are your works! You know me right well.*
> *~ Psalm 139.14*

The ideas included in this book were born out of years of psychotherapy with adoptive and foster children and their families. I was privileged to be their guide on an incredible journey of healing. These are children adopted internationally as early as one year old, adopted domestically after years of abuse, neglect and then foster care, and foster children. The parents and foster parents, dedicated to giving their children a better life, brought them to therapy once and sometimes twice per week for up to three years.

These ideas may run counter to what you think you should do with your child who is no longer an infant and who may even be a toddler or an older child. People in your life such as relatives, friends, pediatricians and social workers may frown upon these methods. You may find yourself alone in your conviction that giving your child and yourself the time and space to just be together, like when a new mother brings her infant home, is the most important thing you can do right now to solidify your child's emotional development. Then this book is for you.

With this book as the vehicle, I will be your mentor to give you the permission, support, encouragement and guidance to insulate you and your newly adopted child from the outside world and to be present in your relationship so you can raise a child to be a person who knows they are valuable, who is capable of having healthy and satisfying relationships, and who is able to be the person they were created to be.

I believe that each of us is "wonderfully made" by God. God has endowed each of us with certain gifts. When we are able to recognize these gifts in ourselves and to see ourselves as a unique creation of God, then we will truly be at peace with ourselves. We will have the best opportunity of discovering and fulfilling the purpose for which we were created.

CHAPTER 1

# *Dreams of Adoptive Parents*

There are as many reasons for adoption as there are parents. You know in your heart why you want to give an orphaned child a home.

You have envisioned yourself as a mother or a father of a beautiful child. You might be parents with biological children who have decided to provide a loving home to one of the many orphaned children in need. Perhaps you have tried for a long time to conceive and for some reason your dream didn't come to fruition. You might have spent years trying infertility treatments to no avail. Perhaps you have lost a child in miscarriage or after birth. You feel that you can't take any more loss and disappointment. "Surely, God desires for me to be a parent," you cry. Your longing seems so unbearable at times. Or, perhaps you have biological children and have discerned a call to bring a neglected and/or abandoned child into your family.

You have been planning this for so long. You have dreamed about your life with your child once you have brought her home. You can just see yourself holding your sweet child as she happily listens to a story you are reading. You expect that your child might take a little while to adjust, but have so much love and joy to offer. You'll shower her with all the love and affection she's been longing for. You'll provide a beautiful, clean home, bountiful meals, friends and family, toys. You'll share your love of God, scripture, prayer and church with her. "She'll come around in no time," you reassure yourself. You're bursting with pride just imagining introducing her to family members and friends; you can see her beaming. Watching your child play with your nieces and nephews, friends' children and the neighborhood children will fill you with joy. You can see yourself watching your child as she rides her tricycle for the first time. If you have children already, you imagine her playing with them or being taken care of by them if they are older.

"Sure, she'll have spunk," you admit. Yes, she'll probably have some adjustment difficulties. It might be difficult to calm her when she's upset. She might not want to sleep in her own bed for a while. She might even ignore you when you reprimand her. Yet, you tell yourself, "She'll just need to get to know us. Once she feels at home and trusts us, she'll come around."

Perhaps you imagine adopting a second child in the future because you want her to have a brother or sister. Running, laughing, riding bikes, playing games together in the yard; you can just see it now. Naturally there will be sibling rivalry between them, but for the most part they will be good companions for each other.

Most adoptive parents have dreams like yours. Most of them have heard the horror stories of those adopted children who, when they become school age, lie, steal, and physically attack their parents. You know this is the extreme and that with your love this can be prevented.

What I have found in my work with adoptive children and parents for the past 13 years is that they are often surprised by the mismatch between the reality of the emotional issues of their adopted child and their dreams. They realize that they are unprepared for the emotional, behavioral and cognitive problems that result from abandonment, living in an orphanage and repeated loss. After years of showering their child with loving relationships and a safe and healthy home they are shocked to discover that their adopted child's problematic behavior won't go away. The problems are chronic and persistent; they continually interfere with relationships in the family and disrupt family routines and activities. Parents and siblings become frustrated, confused, and angry. Feelings of disappointment, regret, and shame crowd out love, patience and acceptance. "What are we doing wrong?" parents ask themselves. Their dreams seem so distant, hardly seeming to have existed at all. Yes, they still love their child dearly, but they need answers, and they need help. Gotcha! was written for you. It is a beginning. Within these pages lie essential and foundational tools both in the form of knowledge and in the form of suggestions for action. Take some slow, deep breaths, put yourself in God's hands and go forward.

CHAPTER 2
# The "Mission" of Adopting an Orphaned Child

You've likely read the statistics. At the time of this publishing, there are more than 130 million orphaned children around the globe due to AIDS, civil war and corrupt governments. Every 2.2 seconds a child loses a parent, and every 15 SECONDS, another child becomes an AIDS orphan in Africa. Although 250,000 children are adopted each year, 14,050,000 children still grow up as orphans and need to live with no place to call home.[1]

In the Ukraine and Russia 10-15% of these children commit suicide before age 18. Sixty percent of the girls become prostitutes and 70% of the boys become criminals.[2] Ten percent of the 100,000 orphans in the Ukraine are orphaned due to death of a parent, the rest are orphaned due to alcoholism, abandonment, or imprisonment of parents.[3]

Harvest Ministry encourages people to realize that there are more orphans in sub-Saharan Africa than all children in Denmark, Ireland, Norway and Sweden, combined. Across the globe approximately 300 million children suffer violence, abuse, child labour, armed conflict, and deplorable situations such as female genital mutilation/cutting and child marriage. Each and every day there are 5,760 new orphans in the world.[4] Another orphan ages out of the orphanage every 2.2 seconds, with no family, no home and nowhere to go.[5]

It is important to understand that children who are left by their biological parents, whether on the steps of a dilapidated building or turned over to an institution such as an orphanage, are "abandoned." Parents are sometimes surprised to be told that even when an infant or child is taken to an orphanage he is "abandoned." They believe this term only refers to infants and children being left alone without any care such as on a street corner or building. Until the baby rests in the arms of a loving "mother" and "father" they will miss having the basic physiological and emotional needs met. The meeting of these needs forges the indispensable foundation upon which all subsequent healthy development depends. Hunger, fear, need for nurturing, illness, or physical discomfort goes unattended until the schedule's allocated time for the related "task." They will, in all likelihood, be left alone to suffer in their distress for extended periods of time.

> **a *ban* don** (verb)
> 1). to leave completely and finally; forsake utterly; desert: *to abandon one's farm.*
> 2). to cast away, leave, or desert, as property or a child: *to abandon a child.*
>
> **forge** (verb)
> 1). to form or make, esp. by concentrated effort: *to forge a friendship through mutual trust.*

One couple described their experience inside the orphanage on their "Gotcha! Day." It was the only time they were permitted near the children's area and it was eerily cold and quiet. Not a cry, not a laugh, no children's voices were heard the whole time they were there. Another couple described the manner in which the diapers were changed in their child's orphanage. In an assembly line set up, each baby in turn was stripped of her diaper, passed to the next worker who, while holding the baby under the arms dipped the baby up and down into a basin of water mixed with sterilizer several times to be passed to the next worker who dried and diapered the baby as if she were wrapping a package of meat.

As long as infants and children live in an institution they rarely experience a warm, loving, smiling face gazing at them while they are held, rocked, fed, sung to, and read to. Many of these children are orphaned so young they spend most of their days lying in a crib.

Children orphaned later in age have experienced this distress for longer periods of time and often have other traumatic experiences. They may have lived in a war-torn village. They may have experienced untold violence. They may have experienced the traumatic death of a parent or sibling. They may have been born into alcoholism or drug addiction, poverty or despair.

Parents who choose to adopt a child are some of the strongest, most impassioned, determined and focused parents I have ever met in 30 years of professional work with families.

Yet perhaps the following sounds familiar: You and your husband have so much love and so many blessings that you have decided to rescue one of these lonely, deprived, orphaned, sweet children. You can make sure he has the love, care, and safety that he was deprived of in his prior life. Yes, by showering your child with all of your love and blessings, he will surely grow emotionally, physically, intellectually, spiritually and socially; he will begin to thrive. By sharing your gifts with him, you will enable him to become the person God created him to be. He will be capable of healthy and satisfying relationships, be a responsible, contributing member of society through career, family and/or serving others and will have a career, raise a family or have a ministry.

Now, you will ensure that his medical, developmental and educational needs will be met. After diligently researching the needs of orphaned children for hours, you have identified the best doctors and services that claim to address these medical issues, developmental delays and gross motor delays that are so common in children who have spent several months to years of their early life in an orphanage in a poverty stricken country. You've gathered recommendations from professionals who have experience with the needs of internationally adopted children such as developmental pediatricians, occupational therapists, and early developmental interventionists. You have connected with support groups of other parents who have adopted children from similar environments. You are ready.

You are committed to do everything you can to insure that you are providing the "best" environment to enable your new, sweet child to be as healthy as possible through and through. You have the phone numbers of the professionals so that you can schedule appointments very soon after you bring your child home. You have been told not to waste a minute—timing is crucial.

It may come as a shock, and may even be unbelievable at this point in your journey, to hear that it is not unusual for parents' well-intentioned and best-laid plans to go awry. What happens? The child doesn't turn out so sweet. Sometimes the child is aggressive, defiant, withdrawn, destructive, or just unable to control their emotions. Parents often try managing these problems themselves. Of course they want their child to avoid the social, emotional and behavioral problems so often associated with children living in orphanages or foster homes, but their best intentions don't keep their child from experiencing serious emotional problems.

In some instances, the child displayed some concerning behaviors, but the parents didn't think they were serious enough to warrant seeking professional help. Parents are often warned about Reactive Attachment Disorder (RAD) and provided with an extensive checklist of symptoms to look out for such as fire setting, cruelty to animals, stealing and property destruction. Some parents will be instructed to seek help from an attachment therapist if their child displays these symptoms.[6]

There are serious problems with the RAD checklist. First of all, it is not grounded in research. Second, many of these symptoms are also symptoms of other problems in children such as Post Traumatic Stress Disorder, ADHD and Depression. Lastly, an adopted child may not display the symptoms on this checklist but display other, more subtle problematic behaviors that may indicate a need for intervention.

Most parents don't notice that anything is wrong for several years after the adoption. They did all of the "right things." They've been to a developmental pediatrician who is an expert in adoption, they've been to the occupational therapist, at least for an evaluation, and they've been to the nutritionist. They have provided the toys and activities that are recommended for their adopted child's age. Their child has attended a wonderful preschool and is possibly preparing to enter kindergarten or first grade. It is not unusual that a second child has joined the family through adoption or birth. Sometimes Mother has decided to return to work.

At some point, parents have a nagging feeling that things just don't seem right. As their child has gotten older these "little" quirks have become a bit more pronounced. They become even more convinced that something is wrong. Their child has frequent temper outbursts with screaming, shutting down, or hitting. It seems that the child gets set off for no reason at all. Nothing the parents have tried calms him down.

The quality of the relationship between the parent(s) and the adopted child just doesn't feel as close and loving as they expected. Stubbornness, particularly at meals, nighttime, and school attendance is frequently a problem. Any disappointment such as not getting a snack when asked for, having to stop a playtime activity, being told "no," not getting enough of Mom or Dad's attention triggers an emotional blow-up. Sometimes the child has difficulty making and/or keeping friends.

The parents are confused. "How could this have happened? We did everything we were told. We've given this child so much love. What did we do wrong?" The primary reason that this happens in my experience is that there are five missing pieces to the puzzle.

The first missing piece is that the emotional nurturing in infancy and the first few years of life, so crucial to later social, emotional and cognitive development, was practically nonexistent for this child prior to adoption. Secondly, it is not uncommon for children who live their first months and years in an orphanage to have what is called Early Relational Trauma (ERT) which affects neurodevelopment, emotional stability, and attachment capabilities.[8] The third is that parenting is hard whether or not your child is adopted. Every member of a family has their own individual temperament with which they were born. It's helpful to understand these differences and the "fit" between parent and child.

The fourth missing piece is about you. What is your attachment history? Do you have any unresolved losses or painful experiences? How good are you at taking care of yourself and managing stress? And lastly is the fifth missing piece: your spiritual/religious history. Empirical evidence is growing to support the positive association between religion and emotional wellbeing. There is also a growing literature base that explains how poor spiritual/religious experiences growing up affect the quality of your relationships, your coping capabilities, and your sense of hope.[9]

The following five chapters will describe each of these missing pieces and the essential part they play in the healthy adjustment of an adopted child.

Throughout the following chapters I have included small exercises called *Stop and Do*. I encourage you to complete each *Stop and Do*. Completing each *Stop and Do*, will enable you to fully benefit from the mentoring I am offering in Gotcha! On the next page you will find your first *Stop and Do*. If you have time now, *Stop and Do* this simple exercise. If you feel rushed, I recommend that you plan some time when you can come back to complete the exercise. Please do not read on until you have completed the *Stop and Do*.

## *Stop and Do*

### Noticing Worries or Concerns

Right now, stop reading and sit quietly for a moment. Listen carefully and notice any worries or concerns you might have for your child. Write them here:

- _____

- _____
  _____

- _____
  _____

We will return to this list in a later in the book.

CHAPTER 3

# The First Missing Piece: Nurturing

When a newborn is brought home from the hospital to join the family, usually Mother and child spend several months together cuddling, sleeping, rocking, feeding, reading, and listening to lullabies. They tend to refrain from a lot of outside activity, choosing to stay home instead. This is, of course, difficult with a family that has older siblings. Often everyone stays home for a period of time instead of running around to appointments, play groups, classes, and other extracurricular activities. This helps the baby become regulated to a routine that works for baby and family.

Most importantly, this kind of nurturing is the best insurance for the development of a healthy, secure attachment for the child. This is essential because a secure attachment is at the root of healthy emotional, social, and cognitive development.[1] A mother and father's warm, sensitive, and responsive interactions with the baby in the first year of life is like sunshine, water, and nutritious soil for a little seedling. It is from such interactions that a secure and healthy sense of self begins to develop.

In the 1950's Harry Harlow, an American psychologist, conducted a series of experiments that provided evidence for the belief that nurturing and love, rather than primarily attending to the infant's physiological needs, are the most important to the healthy development of an infant.[2] It is through nurturing that an infant develops a sense of security rather than fear.  And it is through love that a child develops the sense of trust that is so vital in healthy relationships later in life.

Harlow separated infant monkeys from their mothers a few hours after birth.  He created two different surrogate monkey mothers, both of which offered a constant supply of milk.  One surrogate mother monkey was created out of wire mesh, and the other was covered with a soft terry cloth.  In Harlow's first experiment, he found that when presented with the choice, infant monkeys spent far more time clinging to the terry cloth mothers.  Harlow also discovered that infant monkeys who were restricted to one or the other surrogate mother monkeys behaved significantly different depending on if their surrogate mother monkey provided only for their physiological needs (the wire mesh monkey outfitted with a bottle of milk), or if the surrogate mother monkey provided for their psychological needs of nurturance (the soft terry cloth mother) as well.

Although both sets of monkeys grew physiologically at the same rate, they reacted to frightening experiences in a dramatically different way.  When they were frightened by strange noisy objects like large toy bears beating drums, the monkeys with the choice of a soft terry cloth monkey mother retreated to their surrogate, clinging to them and rubbing against them and eventually calming down.  This cloth, comforting "mother" had become a secure base from which to operate.  Once calm, the monkeys resumed their playful, curious activity.

On the other hand, the monkeys raised with the wire mesh surrogate mother monkeys threw themselves on the floor, rocked back and forth, holding themselves screaming in terror.  Harlow concluded that it was the nurturing that helped the infant monkeys adapt to these threats, and provided a secure base that allowed them to play and explore the world around them.[3]

This research was expanded upon by John Bowlby with the development of his theory of attachment. Bowlby theorized that through many interactions in the first year of life between the primary caregiver and infant, an internal working model of the relationship develops that serves to appraise the safety of relationships and to guide behavior in subsequent relationships. The internal working model is a representation of this first relationship: the caregiver and the infant. The internal working model includes expectations both for what they are worthy to receive from others in relationship and what they expect from others in relationship. If an infant's physical and nurturing needs are only minimally attended to, he will feel unworthy of having his needs met and will have expectations that the "other" in the relationship won't attend to his needs.[4]

### When Newborns and Infants Cry, They Need to Be:

- Held while rocking in a chair or standing
- Offered a bottle
- Gently stroked or patted
- Gently swaddled
- Sung or talked to
- Burped to relieve any trapped gas bubbles
- Gently bathed in warm clean water

A multitude of attachment research, based on Bowlby's attachment theory has demonstrated that when an infant receives sensitive and responsive caregiving during this time, a secure quality of attachment between the child and mother develops.[5] Furthermore, this research has shown us the importance of the attachment relationship to later development. Establishing a secure attachment relationship with their primary caregiver, a child will have the capabilities for healthy and fulfilling relationships, success academically and vocationally, and resiliency in the face of the stresses that life inevitably brings.[6]

D.W. Winnicott, a renowned British psychiatrist, coined the phrase "good enough" mothering.[7] He wanted to help parents understand that children need to have a growing ability to deal with failure and disappointment that inevitably occur over a lifetime. Babies only need "good enough" parenting, not parents trying to be perfect. If parents provide a positive and warm environment fairly consistently, their infant will do just fine even if his parents are unable to do so some of the time. Parents need to be "good enough," not perfect. Children need their parents to be "good enough" in order to learn that they are not the center of everyone's universe.

> The world talks to the mind. Parents speak more intimately -- they talk to the heart.
> ~ Hain Ginott

A mother who typically notices that her infant is expressing a need and seeks to understand this need is exhibiting what is called "sensitive" caregiving. When Mother attempts to soothe her infant by rocking, or nursing, or changing her diaper, she is being "responsive" to her infant's needs. The multitude of tiny nurturing experiences of sensitive and responsive caregiving such as these add up to the child developing a sense of security and trust. Security and trust is the keystone upon which all future development depends. It is through the parents' gentle touch, loving gaze and smile, and playfulness with the child that he begins to develop a sense that he is worthy of being loved, and that he can expect love and care from others with whom he is in relationship. This consistent and reliable external love and security is internalized over time to become the seed of confidence and security in one's self. Most importantly, sensitive and responsive parental interactions are associated with the healthy development of a capacity for handling stress.[8]

When an infant is crying, she is distressed. Mother and Father attempt to calm and soothe their infant by holding him, gently rocking him, offering a bottle or nursing, changing diapers, singing, and touching, to name a few things. As the child becomes a toddler and then a preschooler, Mother and Father help her to calm down through such comforting measures as talking softly, gently hugging, smiling, providing a drink, etc., while offering a comforting object such as a teddy bear or blanket, and the use of distraction. At the same time the parents help the child understand and communicate his emotions by putting words to his feelings. Eventually, the child begins to express his emotions, both pleasant and unpleasant, verbally.

This is how a child learns to tolerate, modulate and regulate their emotions as they grow and develop. First, Mother and Father provide the means of calming. This is later internalized by the child enabling him to develop the capacity to tolerate strong emotions, to regulate them so they don't get out of hand, and to calm himself. This is known as "affect regulation."[9]

When a child experiences chronic lack of emotional sensitivity and responsiveness, a vacuum emerges within. Children who come to our office, whose early months and first years of life were void of these actions of love, have an emptiness inside they cannot describe. They aren't aware this void exists because it is their normal existence. They are like a person who needs glasses, but has lived so long with blurred vision it seems normal. However, the moment an appropriate pair of glasses are placed upon their face, they exclaim in wonderment, "Wow, how clear everything is. I never realized how much I really couldn't see!"

A child who misses out on this vital love in their early life (yes, even in the first few months) actually experience themselves as bad.

This is their experience of themselves, not a thought; they don't have a cognitive or concrete understanding. For them, it is as natural and true as the reality that grass is green, and sugar is sweet, and water is wet. This means that it is not enough for parents to tell them that they are good, or smart, or beautiful. Words are not sufficient nor are they necessary. Actions are both necessary and sufficient. The actions that are offered when your child is distressed are the most impactful.

*Consoling Techniques*

- Rocking, either in a rocking chair or in your arms as you sway from side to side
- Gently stroke his head or pat his back or chest
- Swaddling (wrapping body snugly, but not tightly, in a soft, light blanket)
- Singing or talking
- Playing soft music
- Walking with him in your arms or a stroller
- Riding in the car
- Rhythmic noise and vibration
- A warm bath[1]

Above is a list of consoling techniques that will foster a secure attachment and help your child see you as a source of safety and love. Because your child has more than likely experienced ERT, Early Relational Trauma, (discussed in the following chapter), you will need to be very sensitive to his response to any of these techniques. If you notice a change such as tightening up, looking away, turning away, etc. It may be that he is uncomfortable with what you are doing. I would recommend trying something else.

You may have heard the saying "love is an action, not a

feeling." There is no time in life that this is more true and more crucial than in infancy. The problem is that a child whose early life was spent in an institution such as an orphanage missed this. In order to know inside that they are good and capable and loved, they need to experience love in the way they should have experienced it as an infant. They must experience it now. This is the only sure way they will become a responsible human being, and be able to manage life's disappointments and have healthy relationships.

Relying on words or reasoning or "parenting discipline strategies" with orphaned children is like telling an infant that they don't have to be scared and expecting them to calm down, stop crying and be happy. The child who has missed warm parental love in their infancy needs to experience they are good and valuable and lovable and capable. They need to get this from others in order for them to know this internally.

Unmet, a child's need for this nurturing time does not disappear. I have termed this essential time of nurturing, sheltered from the hubbub of the outside world, between mother and infant Cocooning. It is during this Cocooning period that the self the infant is to become has its birth.

The purpose of this book is to help parents understand the need for Cocooning and how to Cocoon. In later chapters I will introduce the Gotcha! Kits, special kits you may have already purchased with this book or which can be ordered separately at www.NewAdoptionResources.com. The Gotcha! Kit has all the tools you will need for Cocooning. If you'd like to compile your own kit, a list of items included in the Gotcha! Kit is presented in Chapter 11.

Later in this book, I will explain to you how to use the Gotcha! Kit items to help your child to develop a sense of himself as capable, lovable, and valuable, and to develop affect regulation, the capability to tolerate and moderate his emotions. You will also be able to go to our website at www.NewAdoptionResources.com to view videos and our FAQ page to answer questions you might have.

CHAPTER 4
# The Second Missing Piece: Early Relational Trauma

Consider the following scenario: A mother who is incapable of coping with the stress of living in severe poverty with several young children, with no friends or family to help, has a physically abusive husband, or who spends most of her days sleeping, or is unresponsive to the cries of her newborn feels that she must give up on her baby. She cannot find the energy or compassion within herself to comfort this infant - this infant whose body is crying out for her mother's warm breast and loving maternal care. She drags her bundled child to the local church in the middle of the night, leaving her young son on the steps, hoping there he will receive the care she is unable to provide.

Now consider this scenario: In a remote Chinese village, another young mother, gazing upon her second child, a newborn daughter, forces herself to grasp the reality that she had dreaded for nine months. She knows that she has only a few hours, perhaps days, until she has to leave her precious little one in the street to be "found." When her daughter is finally "found" days later, she shows serious signs of prolonged exposure to the 100 degree heat as well as malnutrition.

Once in the orphanage, neither child experiences the loving care so vital to their emotional and physical development, especially in this first year or two of their young life. In the understaffed and underfunded orphanage, which is more like a factory than a home for children, both infants are fed only when the schedule permits it, cleaned when the schedule permits it. They periodically, if ever, feel the comfort of being held by loving arms, the solace of soothing lullabies, or the calming, tender gaze of motherly love. Left in a crib for hours on end with no responses to their cries of distress, these sweet little infants eventually lay quiet and despondent, emotionally cut off at last from their intolerable suffering and grief.

In his seminal book, *Attachment*, John Bowlby, the father of attachment theory, asserted that the quality of maternal caregiving is directly related to the infant's "capacity to cope with stress."[1] About a decade later, researchers began testing out his theory with positive results. Early research indicated that abusive and/or neglectful maternal caregiving in infancy was significantly associated with difficulty in attachment security, stress moderating capabilities and the person's psychological sense of self.[2]

Ever since publishing his attachment theory, scientific evidence for the impact of the quality of attachment experiences on the social emotional well-being of a child has continued to grow. More recent research has shed light on the actual neurological effects of traumatic attachment experiences and what those effects look like in terms of a child's behavior and functioning.

The right hemisphere of the brain is developing during this time (first two years of life). It is dominant for processing, expression and moderation of emotion and is the region of the brain which controls responses to physiological or emotional stress. Caregiving that chronically lacks nurturing, ignores a child's cries, only attending to an infant's physiological needs according to a rigid institutional schedule results in a type of post-traumatic stress disorder, more recently referred to as Early Relational Trauma, as mentioned earlier.[3]

What does Early Relational Trauma really look like in real life? The child who experiences Early Relational Trauma has a profound sense of themselves as "bad," "damaged" and "unlovable." Distress can cause him to become unaware and cut off from his emotions while at the same time his emotions appear out of control.[4] He is unable to identify, moderate, regulate, and express his emotions in an age-appropriate manner. He is carried away by any strong emotion such as sad, angry, disappointment, excitement and his emotions often escalate to the point of disrupting everything and everyone around him.

Eight-year-old Matthew provides an excellent example. He had been begging his parents for a birthday party. His parents knew that all of the children in his elite private school had extravagant birthday parties. "We felt he needed the party or else he would feel embarrassed. We didn't want him to feel different," explained Matthew's adoptive parents.

Matthew's parents were disappointed and embarrassed by Matthew's behavior during the party. "He acted like a selfish, spoiled child," they complained. "He went from gift to gift, almost tossing the opened gift aside to grab for the next gift without barely saying thank you," his parents lamented. "He insisted on being first in line and became mad if the children didn't want to do something his way." Later that evening he hit his sister when she tried to play with one of his new LEGO figures. "We just couldn't understand why he was acting this way when we'd had such a fun day."

Matthew, like many other children who were abandoned and lived in an orphanage during their first year of life, seemed to lack the capability for tolerating disappointment or stress. Often the disappointment or stress is imperceptible to anyone else.

Matthew's behavior exemplifies Early Relational Trauma

manifesting later in childhood. Instead of the joy and appreciation his mother expected, Matthew was angry, rejecting, aggressive and defiant.

For children with Early Relational Trauma social and emotional excitement and overstimulation often triggers painful emotionally-charged body memories stemming from the early traumatic attachment experiences. When these physiological and/or emotional traumatic memories are provoked, the nervous system automatically goes into fight or flight mode: the child reacts either by withdrawing or acting out.[5] During this automatic reaction, the child (or adult for that matter) is operating out of a primitive area of the brain which is ruled by emotion and reflex only, called the amygdala. When operating out of this area of the brain, thinking through a situation rationally and problem solving is impossible. Matthew's behavior exhibited this kind of thinking when he became easily angered and even aggressive.

A child experiencing this feels that his needs are unimportant to those around him. Parents and other adults usually view his negative behavior as manipulative, defiant and disrespectful. Although this view is understandable and logical, it is mistaken. Rather, the child is experiencing intense psychological distress at exposure to internal or external cues that resemble an aspect of his early relational trauma. Usually the child is unaware of this internal psychological distress. If you asked him what happened or what upset him, he would not know. He is unaware that he is experiencing a trauma reaction of terror, confusion, and despair - it is the only way he can express his needs.

The second characteristic of Early Relational Trauma is dissociation.[6] When an infant, and later a child, is abandoned and then regularly left unattended, the distress this causes is often more than he can bear. Our mind has been created in such a way that in such circumstances it just shuts out overwhelming emotional and/or physical distress from consciousness. Dissociation is the separation of whole segments of the personality or parts of the self from consciousness.

For infants, this type of prolonged distress is particularly harmful because all they know is the here and now. They cannot think to themselves, "This will end soon; it will not last forever." As a result, such prolonged distress is experienced as life threatening and results in feelings of terror. The infant and child's mind eventually shuts off from these distressing emotions and this develops into "dissociation."[7]

James and Joyce Roberston, students of John Bowlby's, filmed young children institutionalized in England in the 1960's. As was the custom at the time, children were institutionalized while the mother was hospitalized. Often the child stayed at the institution for about two weeks and the father visited occasionally.

Analyzing the children's response to the father's departure over the two week period, John Bowlby and the Robertsons found that on average the children went through three distinct phases during this separation. First, the child was very distressed, crying and calling often for his parents. This is the "protest" phase. Secondly, the child experienced periods of tearfulness and sadness. This is the "despair" phase.[8] Lastly, the child became despondent, with no crying or overt distress. This is the "detachment" phase.[5] It is during this detachment phase that the infant is psychologically shut off from awareness of the anxiety-provoking information. Detachment is a defense against feeling the anxiety which is associated with the earlier traumatic distress due to abandonment and life in an institution.

> Each day of our lives we make deposits in the memory banks of our children.
> ~ Charles R. Swindoll

The defense of "detachment" can, at times, act as dissociation, which is the loss of awareness of thoughts, feelings, and experiences. There are two ways in which a child will react when they have an experience that somehow triggers a physiological or emotional memory of the distress they experienced as a result of abandonment and living in an institution. The child may withdraw or act out angrily and/or aggressively toward others or himself. When this happens, the withdrawal or aggression, as well as the provoking situation, is often outside of the child's conscious awareness.

## Neurobiology of Early Relational Trauma

Andrew was adopted at the age of 12 after being raised by his father who had physically and sexually abused him most of his early life. Cindy and her husband Mark had been working hard in treatment putting to use Bruce Perry M.D.'s model of Adaptive Responses to Threat[9] along with the missing pieces of nurturing and trauma. These concepts are presented to parents of adoptive and foster children in the parent collaboration component of our treatment model.

"He blew up in school again," Andrew's mother complained. "I don't know what sets him off, but the principal wants him out. He's fine at home, I just don't know what to do. This last time he threw his books at the teacher and flipped his desk over. Then he refused to talk with anyone. He just shut down. The principal called and told us he was suspended. I picked him up right away." Cindy looked worried and was desperate to help her 12 year old son. Andrew was adopted domestically just about six months prior to this incident and the family had been working hard to help fill in the missing pieces.

"Do you ever see this behavior at home?" I queried.

"We saw it fairly often when Andrew first came to live with us, but that was two months ago. Now he might get mad suddenly, but he just shuts down. Then we know he's upset about something."

"What happens then?"

"I usually go to him and just sit with him. Speaking softly and gently I tell him I'd like to hear about what is bothering him, and that I'd like to help him if he can tell me. He usually doesn't say anything, and he looks like he hates me. He won't even look at me.

But, I just stay with him, sitting off to the side. Eventually he softens, looking like a vulnerable, shy, 10 year old boy. Then he'll approach me gingerly and sit next to me. As I put my arm around his shoulders, he turns in to me and begins to cry. I put my other arm around him and he collapses in my arms and begins to sob."

Cindy continued, "I just hold him gently for a while and then tell him I'm sorry he is hurting so much inside. I tell him I love him and that I'm glad he let me hold him." Now I'm not saying that he responds that way every time, but that is more common now than is an all-out temper tantrum."

The Bruce Perry, M.D. model of Adaptive Responses to Threat explains the "fight or flight" response we all have when a threat is perceived. It is also known as the autonomic nervous system, which includes the sympathetic nervous system and the parasympathetic nervous system. The former is our gas peddle and the latter is our neurological brake pedal.

The fight or flight response is an automatic physiological response that we were created with to insure our safety when we are threatened. Adrenaline is pumped into the blood stream which transports it to our brain. Organs that aren't essential to survival tend to shut down and our organs essential to survival go into hyperdrive. The heart rate increases, breathing becomes more rapid, our muscles become energized. Our brain begins functioning out of the limbic, or emotional and reactive part of the brain. As the higher thinking regions of the brain (the cortex) shuts down, the command center is handed over to the more primitive regions of our brain: the limbic system and the brain stem. When these regions are in control, all reactions are emotional and reflexive, a person has no sense of time, and thoughts concerned with what is happening or how to solve the problem go right out the window. We have no rational thinking at this time and no planning ability.

Why is this so important in relation to a child with Early Relational Trauma? First of all, a child with Early Relational Trauma will often perceive a threat when no one else is aware that anything is at all threatening. Because the original trauma occurred pre-verbally, and often within the first year of life, the child has no conscious memory of the trauma. He also is unaware of feeling a perceived threat.

For anyone who has experienced any sort of trauma and suffers Post Traumatic Stress Disorder, they too will experience perceived threat. The difference between this person and the child with Early Relational Trauma is that the child with ERT will more than likely never have any verbal memories of the exact circumstances of the trauma. This makes healing more difficult.

Let's take Andrew as an example. He remembers his trauma and abuse. However, he is unaware of the environmental stimuli that causes him to sense threat. His reaction begins autonomically.

Imagine you are leisurely walking down the street on a warm, sunny day. You hear the birds singing and the spring leaves rustling in the gentle breeze. All of a sudden you hear a horn blowing and car brakes screeching behind you. Your heart begins to beat faster, you quickly look back to see what is happening. You might even find that you jumped to the side or froze in your spot. Your fight or flight response, your autonomic nervous system, has been activated. You are now in the aroused state and your cognitive functioning has moved to a lower region of the brain. You don't hear the birds or the leaves anymore. Your sense of time has decreased from months and years to hours and days.

If the car stops and you have determined that all is safe, you resume your walk. Soon your heart slows down and you are aware of the birds chirping again. However, if the car has not stopped, but continues careening towards you, you then move into a state of alarm and eventually terror.

As you move along this continuum of fight or flight, command central has now moved to the most primitive area of your brain. Your sense of time is now limited to the present moment and you can only react reflexively. This is purely physiological.

What is the implication of this physiological change? You are acting without thinking. You are unable to think through the situation. Trying to implement any problem solving model you've read about is impossible.

This is what happens to a child with Early Relational Trauma. And remember, most of the trauma occurred within relationship. As a result, it will be behavior of others with whom the child is in relationship that will often trigger a sense of perceived threat. This could be something as subtle as a tone of voice, a touch, a gesture, a smell. It could also be environmental such as recalling sounds, time of day, taste, tiredness, illness. You cannot know and will often be perplexed by the triggers that a child perceives as threatening.

What you can know is that your child's behaviors can tell you what is triggering the reaction. And these triggers are actually clues to the unknown puzzle pieces of your child's early life. When you begin to understand what the child perceives as threatening, you can understand the trauma that she experienced as an infant prior to abandonment by her birth mother, during the abandonment, and her life in the orphanage. Awareness of this is painful. When we are willing to look and to see what is there, we will come face to face with the sad hard truth of this child's legacy of loss and neglect. See it we must, if we are to be a healing presence for this child.

CHAPTER 5

# The Third Missing Piece: Parenting is Hard!

This is a missing piece that I find is often helpful to many adoptive parents. They are so used to attributing everything to the adoption. Sometimes, it is the child's personality. Sometimes, it is typical frustrations of parenting.

When we recognize that all children, and even adults, are always growing up on the inside, it helps put things into perspective. If we are honest with ourselves, we will recognize that pain and suffering is an inherent ingredient in this growing up process. Growth comes with growing pains. Without them, we will not grow.

In recognizing and accepting the formidable nature of raising an orphaned child, as well as the strength and willingness to change on your part, you become a healthier, more mature adult. Your relationships in general will improve, and you will heal your own wounds from the past.

When my son was just a toddler, I was lamenting to a friend about a discipline struggle. She asked me, "Whatever made you think that parenting should be easy?" I have never forgotten that question. When I struggle now as a parent, I remember my friend's comments and it brings me right back to reality. It brings me right back to acceptance of what is. It brings me to a place of peace.

If you do not have biological children, you may have a tendency to view your parenting struggles through the lens of adoption or attachment. It can be of utmost benefit to you to remind yourself that the struggles may, in fact, be "normal" or "typical" parenting experiences that even happen to parents raising biological children. This is called "normalizing."

All of the struggles you experience with your adopted child are not due to the adoption. Sometimes the struggles may be due to parenting, your own personal family history, your temperament, your child's temperament, any mismatch between the two, and the child's developmental struggle between striving for autonomy and fear of separation from Mother and Father.

As long as parents have expectations that parenting "should" be a certain way or that their child "should" act a certain way, they will frequently be disappointed and even exasperated. I have heard it said that the amount of serenity a person experiences in any relationship is inversely related to the amount of expectations they have for that relationship.

We can vastly improve the quality of any relationship just by letting go of expectations, imagining placing the person into God's hands, and accepting the person for whom God created them to be. Before going on to read about temperament, complete the *Stop and Do: Becoming Aware of Expectations*.

## Temperament

We are all born with our temperament. You've probably heard of the nature vs. nurture debate about how we come to be the way we

## Stop and Do

### Becoming Aware of Expectations

Right now, stop reading and sit quietly for a moment. Be aware of your breathing. Close your eyes and breathe gently in and out once for every letter of your name. Now, think about your adopted child and ask yourself what expectations you have of him. Be honest with yourself and write them down here:

1). _____

2). _____

3). _____

Now that you are aware of these expectations, it is important to let go of them. Imagine yourself offering them to God. Now, for each expectation, write a statement of acceptance of who your child is.

1). _____

2). _____

3). _____

are; how our personality develops. Psychology now concedes that it is both nature (what we are born with) and nurture (our upbringing and other environmental factors) that determine why we are who we are.

The nature part is called temperament. Thomas and Chess first introduced their New York Longitudinal Study in 1952, in which they identified nine temperament traits.[1]

Through their research, Thomas and Chess determined that we are born with our temperament and live with it for the rest of our lives. In other words, our temperamental traits are stable throughout our lifetime and do not change as a result of circumstances and experiences.[2]

As mentioned previously, many adoptive parents have a tendency to attribute all of their adopted child's difficult behaviors to the fact that they were adopted. However, the difficulty may in fact be due to the child's temperament, and/or a mismatch between the child and parent's temperament. Here are the nine temperament traits according to Chess and Thomas:

- **Activity:** Is the child constantly active or more relaxed?
- **Rhythmicity:** Is the child regulated in terms of sleeping and eating, or more chaotic?
- **Approach/withdrawal:** Does the child move toward new objects and/or people easily, or tend to shy away?
- **Adaptability:** Does the child seem to be flexible or rigid when changes occur?
- **Intensity:** Is the child's reactions (either negative or positive) intense or calm?
- **Mood:** Is the child's mood generally negative or positive, erratic or even?
- **Persistence and attention span:** Is the child persistent or does he give up easily?
- **Distractibility:** Is the child easily distracted or is he able to stick with the activity despite distractions?

- **Sensory threshold:** Is he bothered by sensory stimuli such as noise, texture or is he unbothered by them?

## Understanding Temperament Helps Parents to:

- become aware of your child's temperament, accept your child as he is, and refrain from comparing your child to others.
- become aware of your own temperament, and strive to use this information to help you improve the quality of intimacy between you and your child.
- understand and respect the differences between your temperament and that of your child's.
- enjoy the interaction between your temperament and that of your child's.
- set clear limits according to your child's temperament.
- prevent melt-downs in your intense child by decreasing intense and unexpected experiences.

It will be helpful to familiarize yourself with Thomas and Chess' nine temperamental traits and to identify where your child falls on each of the traits on the scale from mild to intense. This will help you to better understand your child. Instead of trying to change behaviors that are really inherent to the specific traits, and therefore God-given, you can work *with* them.

When you identify your own traits you can determine whether you have a "good enough" fit with your child. If you and your child's level of intensity on any of the temperament traits are out of sync, you will probably be experiencing greater struggle in your relationship. Understanding this difference will help to minimize these struggles.

In her book, *Raising the Spirited Child*, Sheila Kurcinka helps parents to discover their child's temperamental style and offers parenting styles that are most effective for each.[3] Take your time and complete the *Stop and Do: Temperament Rating Scale* at this time.

Return to your list worries and/or concerns from the *Stop and Do* at the end of Chapter 2. Comparing the items on your list to your responses on this scale, determine if you can understand the concerns and/or worries any better. Does your child's temperament help to explain some of your items?

## Stop and Do

### Temperament Rating Scale

Right now, stop reading and sit quietly for a moment. Be aware of your breathing. Now, rate your child on the nine traits of temperament by circling the number, then rate yourself. Identify matches and mismatches, and be aware of this in your relationship.

**Activity**
(Mild)  1  2  3  4  5  6  7  8  9  10  (Intense)

**Rhythmicity**
(Mild)  1  2  3  4  5  6  7  8  9  10  (Intense)

**Approach/Withdrawal**
(Mild)  1  2  3  4  5  6  7  8  9  10  (Intense)

**Adaptability**
(Mild)  1  2  3  4  5  6  7  8  9  10  (Intense)

**Intensity**
(Mild)  1  2  3  4  5  6  7  8  9  10  (Intense)

**Mood**
(Mild)  1  2  3  4  5  6  7  8  9  10  (Intense)

**Persistence/Attention Span**
(Mild)  1  2  3  4  5  6  7  8  9  10  (Intense)

**Sensory Threshold**
(Mild)  1  2  3  4  5  6  7  8  9  10  (Intense)

CHAPTER 6

# The Fourth Missing Piece: You

Yes, you. Ask yourself, these questions: "How was I nurtured by my parents?" "Was I nurtured by my parents?" "If not my parents, was there another adult such as a grandparent, aunt, or family friend who provided you with love and security?" "How were my attachment needs met?" "Am I nurturing and kind to myself?" Learning what you have about attachment in the previous chapters, do you believe that you received what you needed from your parents in order to be okay with who you are, to feel your inherent worth and value?

Awareness, or the lack thereof, of your own attachment experiences will impact how you parent. Many people have had poor attachment experiences and are in need of healing. Remember, our attachment style is formed in the first year of life and as long as there is no dramatic change in our parents' behavior, it is reinforced through those relationship interactions. If we had an insecure attachment style there is hope. John Bowlby said that although attachment styles are resistant to change, change is possible with repeated positive relationship experiences.[1]

Repeated positive relationship experiences are healing and help us to relate to others with greater authenticity and as a result, more intimately. Look at your relationships with family and friends. Spend more time with those who are kind and loving, and less time with those who are critical and/or self focused.

When parents have insecure attachments, it is the lack of awareness of the quality of your own attachment experiences that affect the quality of your relationships with your children. As a result of this lack of awareness, you will interact with others, especially your children, habitually out of these old attachment experiences. You will recreate the same, negative attachment relationships with your children and you won't know why or how this happened.

Awareness is the beginning of change. There will be things about your child or your relationship that will provide you with an opportunity to look honestly at yourself. Utilize such tools as writing in a journal, reading, or talking with a trusted friend. Psychotherapy is a helpful way to examine these significant attachment experiences and the impact they have had on your own life. This will be healing and transforming. It will give you the ability to create the kind of relationships you desire, *especially* with your child.

I believe your children, however challenging, were given to you because God believes you are the best parents to raise them. You are the parents your child needs to become who God created her to be. As much as our children need us, I also believe that our children, however challenging, were given to us to help us become the person we were created to be.

CHAPTER 7
# The Fifth Missing Piece: God

A healthy relationship and reliance on God is essential to anyone's emotional well-being. And, even more important says the research, religion significantly contributes to our emotional well-being and our ability to cope with stress. Religion has also been found to decrease depression and to positively affect one's ability to cope with anxiety, trauma and PTSD symptoms.[1]

What is your view of God? Do you view Him as harsh and distant, or as kind, firm, and loving? Do you trust that He cares about you and helps you? Perhaps you do not believe in God at all.

Our attachment relationships significantly impact our view of God and the quality of our relationship with God.[2] Your view of God and the quality of your relationship with God will impact your children's relationship with God. "Is this really important to helping my child adjust to her new life with us?" you might ask.

Take a look at this image. This is an icon painting called "Our Lady Of Perpetual Help," first painted in Crete in the late 15th century.

This is a painting of Jesus as a child with his mother, Mary.

In the upper portion of the icon, the two angels are carrying the instruments of Jesus' passion and death. In Jesus' human nature, as he is depicted here, he is frightened and runs to his mother for safety and protection. She quickly picks him up and holds him tightly against her. She holds him close and leans her head toward him. Jesus' fear is apparent in his clasp of his mother's hand and in his right foot twisted nervously around the other. He fearfully gazes at the angels. He ran to his mother in such haste that he almost lost the sandal dangling from his right foot. Yet, Mary's face is calm and full of compassion for Jesus in His fear and sorrow. She offers Jesus safety - she is His *safe haven*, His *secure* base.

This is an excellent depiction of a secure, healthy attachment. When a child is afraid, his Mother is sensitive and responsive to his needs. In this icon, Our Lady of Perpetual Help is sensitive to Jesus' fear and sorrow, which we can see on her face; she responds by staying calm and protectively holding Him. This is the relationship we can have with God. When we are afraid, worried, or nervous, we can turn to Him and trust in His love and care for us. We can have hope and faith that He is sensitive to our distress and our needs, and that He does respond. This provides us with strength. When you have this trust, hope, and faith in God and you see God as your lover, guide, and protector, your child will be more likely to have a similar relationship with God.

For you, as the parent, this means one of two things: If you have a healthy spirituality and religiosity, turn to God for guidance, support, and strength just as Jesus turned to His mother in the icon. I encourage you to turn to the spiritual practices inherent to your religion. I also encourage you to turn to fellow congregants and ministers and/or priests. However, , if you don't have a strong faith and are not active in a religion, perhaps this is the time to return. Make a decision to talk with a spiritual advisor such as a minister, priest, or spiritual director about your resistance, questions, and/or past uncomfortable experiences with faith and religion. It will be helpful if you move beyond this place so that you can rely on God and your faith as a source of strength.

There is another reason that discovering or re-discovering a faith and religion is also important at this time. In doing so, you will give your child an additional source of strength and positive self-image to help him through the struggles that are a part of his adoption journey.

Your child needs to know that he is "wonderfully made" by God, is loved by God, was created by God. He needs to know that he can talk to God when he is alone and trust that God hears him. He needs to know, when he is ready, that his biological parents are in God's hands, and that God brought him to you for protection. He needs to know that all of these things are not random and that it is God's wish for him to experience love, peace and joy. He needs to know that God created him and has desires for him, and in time, with healing, he can come to know these desires. All of this will help to answer the questions that all adopted children have: *Was I abandoned because I was defective? Why didn't God protect me?* And you, my friend, are the one who will show this to him in your actions and in your words.

CHAPTER 8
# Cocooning Part 1: What & Why?

What is Cocooning™? The best example of Cocooning is what we often see when observing mothers with their first born infants. During the first few months with a new infant, Mother often stays home with her infant, getting to know her newborn. Here are some questions a mother of a new infant usually asks herself during this time:

- How long does my baby sleep at any given time?
- Does she seem most relaxed when closely held and cuddled, when she is lying on my lap or in the cradle?
- Does she cry intensely, frequently, and for long periods or more softly, less frequently, and shorter duration?
- How reactive is she to environmental stimuli such as bright light, sounds, touch, air temperature?
- How reactive is she to sudden changes in environmental stimuli?
- Does she appear to calm when I sing to her, rock her, play, or talk to her?

This early time together allows Mother to adjust to her infant's temperament and schedule. At this time of development, the mother is the infant's world. Symbiosis is the psychological term that describes this lack of differentiation between the infant and her mother.[1] In the infant's experience, they are one. Mother and baby are one. The more frequently Mother and infant are together during this time, the healthier the child will be.

The newborn learns to regulate herself with Mother's help. As Mother learns what calms her baby, holding her firmly against her chest, rocking her in her arms, singing to her, etc., the infant is slowly learning how to do this for herself. In doing this, parents act as a "container" for the infant which helps the baby begin to learn to tolerate and regulate internal affect. It begins here in infancy and is slowly internalized throughout childhood. We saw a great example of this in the previous chapter in the icon of Mary holding Jesus. By providing this safe container, Mary helped Jesus tolerate and regulate his overwhelming fear.

Attachment forms within the first year of life. For this reason, this is the time for mother to be sensitive and responsive to her infant's needs *most* of the time. This is the crucial time for the development of a sense of trust and security that will form the foundation of all later social, emotional, and cognitive development.[2] This is Cocooning.

The manner in which a parent provides a "container" changes according to the developmental age of the child. However, the most important foundation is laid in infancy through the end of the first year of life. As the baby becomes more aware of the world around her, she begins to explore away from mother. At first she explores with her eyes and hands and then, as she becomes more mobile, she begins to crawl and explore further. The security and trust she has had with her mother is directly related to the extent to which she will explore and learn about the world around her. Her mother is her secure base from which she explores the world around her.

You might not think your adopted child needs Cocooning if

she was adopted after the first few months of birth. However, this is a mistaken notion. Whatever you don't know about your child's intrauterine life, birth, and infancy, you do know that your child missed out on Cocooning during infancy. Cocooning with your child after you first bring her home provides you with vital information about her needs, emotions and perceptions (or misperceptions) about the world. Cocooning requires time and willingness.

You will need time and willingness to learn about your child's behavior and consider what this behavior can inform you about your child's needs. Most likely your child has needs that were never attended to as an infant. By being sensitive to the child's behavior and by trying to understand the child—the hidden child—you will be able to figure out your child's unmet needs. You will be able to intervene proactively, rather than reactively. Eventually you will be able to teach and model appropriate ways for your child to express her needs and emotions and to check out the accuracy of her perceptions.

The purpose of parenthood is to insure the child's safety and to help her become the person God created her to be. For your child to grow up on the inside and become the person God created her to be you must provide her with a secure base. From this secure base, the child learns that the world is safe, she learns that they are loved and worthy, and that she has a solid foundation from which to explore the world around her. She will learn to expect that others are usually kind as opposed to expecting others will disregard and abandon her.

A child who has experienced Early Relational Trauma does not mature emotionally in sync with their chronological age. Therefore, we need to determine the emotional age at which the child is functioning. This is important because the child has missed out on experiences that are essential building blocks of development.

Think of development as a structure that is built one block upon another. If one block is missing, the structure will collapse. We must fill in the missing building blocks. So, we ask the question: "At what age would this behavior be typical?" Usually the answer is age two or less. I have found this to be true whether the child is four or six or fourteen.

An example is James, a six year old boy domestically adopted from foster care. Cindy, his adoptive mother, was constantly frustrated because he would take forever to eat dinner. When she left him to get dressed for school, he was always distracted and was never able to do it without her constant prodding. If left alone in a room, he would get into trouble by pulling plants off the window sill or sticking items into the DVD player. After instructing him to get dressed for school in the morning, his exasperated mother would return thirty minutes later to find him playing instead of getting dressed as she told him to.

Contemplating at what age these behaviors would be typical, Cindy decided that he was emotionally a two-year-old. She began to adjust her expectations for his behavior to those she *would* have if her son were two years old. She no longer left him alone; she now expected that he would eat only small bits of food at meals and need assistance dressing himself. She now supervised him at *all* times. Instead of becoming angry when he misbehaved, she calmly explained to him that this was wrong, gently telling him what he should be doing.

Most importantly, she nurtured James the way a two year old needs to be nurtured. She read to him at night, she frequently cuddled with him, and she provided playthings that a younger child would enjoy. She let him play with toys in the bathtub, she took him for walks, played fingerplays with him and provided more time for play. They went to parks and playgrounds; he loved swinging. She kept him home from school for a year, providing him with natural experiential learning experiences. Basically, she spent a lot of time with him, enjoying him and loving him.

Cindy was relieved when she began to see James' problem behaviors decreasing. After many months, she realized that he was beginning to mature on the inside. She could now leave him alone to get dressed and come back in ten minutes to find him dressed. She found that he didn't need as much prodding to accomplish simple tasks as he did previously. Now he was no longer two, but seemed to be acting like a four year old. Cindy realized that now she needed to respond to him as if he were a four year old. She needed to change her expectations again so what she expected of him matched the abilities of a four year old.

As Cindy adjusted her expectations accordingly, she continued to see James grow up on the inside until he seemed to behave pretty close to his chronological age. He continued to have times when he would have a severe reaction to something like a significant change or disappointment, but now Cindy and I could work together to help James learn tools that he could use to help *himself* cope in similar situations.

Why Cocooning? Cocooning will help you and your child develop a positive, secure attachment relationship which is a major building block for healthy cognitive and emotional development. Children with more secure attachment relationships with their parents learn more easily, get along better with peers and manage conflict better than children who do not have secure attachment relationships with their parents.[2]

Cocooning is the time when mother and baby are like one; it is a vital experience for the beginning of the development of a healthy person. During this time you provide the child with experiences of safe and appropriate interactions that engender a sense of safety, trust and well-being. Cocooning will help your child begin to experience you as a safe haven.

Just as a mother of a newborn needs time to get to know her newborn, so does an adoptive mother need time to get to know her child. Babies are born with their own temperament, their own rhythm. In their research as mentioned earlier, Chess and Thomas identified three basic temperaments: easy, difficult, and slow to warm up.[3] Cocooning provides you with the opportunity to become familiar with your individual child, for you to learn about your baby's temperament and to discover the personality God gave your child.

***Key: Secure attachment relationships develop through thousands of tiny, simple interactions between Mother and child (and Father and child).***

## Cocooning...

- Facilitates opportunities for positive and healing attachment experiences
- Decreases overstimulation and triggering trauma reactions
- Best way to begin child's healing and growth developmentally, emotionally and cognitively
- Helps parents become familiar with child
- Helps parents establish family routines based on family, personality of child, health of child

CHAPTER 9

# Cocooning Part II: How?

Remember, the two factors most associated with the development of security are sensitivity to what needs the child is expressing and responding in an appropriate way to those needs.¹ The child will act according to his own expectations of what he deserves and these expectations are formed from their early relational experiences within the first year of life², usually with their biological parents and to the caregivers in the orphanage or foster home. Your job in Cocooning is to help change these expectations by sensitive and responsive actions.

In all your interactions, especially during this Cocooning time, remember to be sensitive and responsive.

## Creating a Safe Haven

When you first bring your child home, he will need a safe haven to buffer him from all of the new and exciting people, situations, places and things. He will be easily overwhelmed. If you've ever moved to a new city or state, you'll have a glimpse of what he's experiencing.

When everything is novel for a child, when he's been cut off from everything that is familiar, the baseline of his state of arousal will be high. This means that he will be easily triggered into a terror state with the potential to shut down or explode. Staying home as much as possible will help minimize this. You and your home need to be a *safe haven* for him. This means that, if possible, one parent stays home as long as possible after your Gotcha! Day. This will make a huge difference in the quality of your safe haven.

Cocooning during this time when you are at home together, minimizing novelty and outside activity, being close, will help decrease unexpected outbursts. Cocooning will help your child to eventually feel comfortable with all of the strangers who comprise his new family. He will eventually become familiar with the strange and possibly frightening surroundings that make up his new home.

At first, spend as much of your time in as few rooms of your home as possible. Try to take your meals in one area and spend the rest of the time in another, perhaps in his room or in the family room. If you have other children, regularly spending time alone with your new one while another parent or caregiver takes care of siblings elsewhere is recommended during this time.

Another way to create a safe haven is through ritual. Ritual is defined by Dictionary.com as "any practice or pattern of behavior regularly performed in a set manner." This external regularity is instrumental for children learning to regulate their affect. The goal of this external regulation is for it to be internalized, enabling the child to modulate and regulate a wide range of affect. Regular mealtimes, prayers, reading aloud time, fingerplay time, naptime, celebrating birthdays and significant holidays, attending church are all types of rituals.

Repetitive activities using the same materials, in the same

locations, at the same times of day provides simple rituals that help children build a sense of security and safety. Create rituals for your child and your family as much as you can. Below is a list of great activities for building a secure base. They can become wonderful, memorable rituals that help create a safe haven for your child. Later in this chapter, this list is elaborated with specific directions and guidelines for Cocooning.

### Perfect Activities for Building a Secure Base:

- Cuddling time (rocking chair, soft blankets/throws, large pillows, stuffed animals)
- Invite your child to have a "snuggly" or "blankie"
- Provide a baby bottle and/or pacifier
- Reading aloud (fairy tales, Caldecott Winner books), board books and picture books together
- Have board books around for child to look through at their leisure
- Listen to music (lullabies, classical, children's folk songs) together
- Water toys and books for bath time along with taking baths
- Outside playtime together at home and/or playground; explore nature together
- Walks using a stroller or wagon
- Follow American Pediatric Association recommendations for TV and video viewing for 0 - 2 year olds (which is none)
- Obtain a copy of *I Love You Rituals* by Becky A. Bailey, Ph.D. and her CD, *Songs for I Love You Rituals*

During Cocooning you are child-centered and are moving along with your child. This means you have to be quiet, calm and present with your child. Thoughts about what you should be doing and what your child should be doing will flood your mind. These are expectations and they are messages coming from others in your family, friends and society. When they appear, just notice them and then let them go. Imagine yourself handing them over to God or putting them in a box and setting the box on a shelf. This is the crucial time for your child to begin the process of experiencing acceptance and love as he is, not as someone else wants him to be.

As mentioned previously, when you practice being present with your child in whatever activity you engage in, you'll more than likely be flooded with the "shoulds." Although this is usually true for most new parents, this is even more true for parents of adopted children. Your child will, in all likelihood, have experienced deprivation of motor movement, holding, visual stimuli, verbal stimuli and toys in their previous home. Such deprivation usually results in some degree of developmental delay. Most adoptive parents feel a strong responsibility to help their child fill in the developmental gaps so that they function at their chronological age. They will feel pressured to teach, provide stimulating activities, and push the child along.

Others may criticize or just simply question your parenting. It is not your job to satisfy them. During this early time with your child, it is your job to get to know your child and to build a secure attachment. This is the foundation that all further development is built upon. It must be formed patiently, with care, deliberateness, and thoroughness. The first step is to "shoo away the shoulds." At this time complete the *Stop and Do: Shooing Away the "Shoulds."*

## Details of Cocooning

Our culture encourages parents to teach their children. More often than not, parent interactions with their children center around helping them to learn, to become obedient, to be responsible and to

## Stop and Do

**Shooing Away the "Shoulds"**

1). Gently stop whatever you are doing.

2). Sit quietly, close your eyes and take three slow calm breaths all the way into your abdomen and gently out through your mouth.

3). With your eyes closed and still breathing fully and gently, ask God to put a loving, gentle reminder in your thoughts.

4). When you have the words, write them down.

_____
_____
_____
_____

5). During cocooning time, when negative, critical thoughts enter your mind, stop, take a few deep, gentle breaths and say your reminder. Say it to yourself, remembering to breathe gently, until you feel relaxed and fully present in the moment.

be courteous. While these are important tasks of raising children, these are not the interactions that build secure attachments. These types of interactions are what Cocooning *isn't*.

Let's return again to our example of a mother bringing home her newborn infant. Most developmental psychologists and pediatricians agree that the primary task for an infant's first year of life is the development of security and trust. They also agree that in order to do this, parents need to meet their child's needs most of the time up to the first year of life.

Most adopted children do not experience security and trust at all prior to their Gotcha! Day. As this is the fundamental building block for all subsequent development, they need to have this experience. Therefore, no matter what your adopted child's age at the time of adoption, your interactions need to involve acceptance, validation, safety, healthy limits and love. These types of interactions will help build a secure attachment relationship between you and your child. These are also the types of interactions that help to heal the deep neural and emotional wounds that are the fallout from early relational trauma. These types of interactions are Cocooning.

## Guidelines for Cocooning

Here are five guidelines to help you understand how to Cocoon:

**1). Cuddle or be in close proximity to your child.** During Cocooning, and depending on your child's activity, you can either cuddle with your child or just sit in close proximity to him. Cuddle only if your child is receptive to your gesture. If he is looking at a book or some other quiet activity, cuddle. If he is playing, or doesn't seem comfortable with your gesture to cuddle, sit in close proximity. Sharon, the mother in the next example, chose to sit in close proximity. Look at your child's face to see if he is looking at you. If so, make eye contact and smile. What you do next depends on him. Follow his lead, letting him be your guide, but be sure to read and use all of these guidelines. We'll talk more about letting your child be your guide when we discuss Guideline number five.

Cocooning might entail that you pull your child gently onto your lap while you sit in a soft rocking chair and read aloud (be sure to follow guidelines 1-4 when reading aloud). It might be listening to children's folk songs and dancing around the room together. It might be filling a large bin with water and giving plastic containers and measuring cups to your child to use (Be sure to have some towels on hand!). Later, we'll talk more about specific Cocooning activities.

Positive attachment experiences do not always have to entail touching. An intimate connection can be made physically as in cuddling or with proximity and/or eye contact. What is important is what your child is comfortable with in *this* moment. Be sensitive; work on discerning what your child might like. Then, be responsive; provide what you think he would be comfortable with in this particular moment. He'll let you know if you've hit the mark or not. It is also important, if your child typically wants to be very close, but is playing contentedly while you sit at a little distance, to just let him be. This will help your child experience a sense of security concurrently with a little separation.

**2). Observing and listening; just be present with your child.** Are you fully present with your child? If you're like most of us, your answer will be no. So often, in any given moment in our day, we are thinking about something that happened yesterday and about what we have to cook for dinner tonight. We might be overwhelmed by our "to do" list or the argument we had yesterday with a good friend - anything but the present moment. We can be present by taking a few minutes to focus on our breathing and to notice any sounds, sights, and physical feelings that are surrounding us in that very moment.

When you are present with your child, you are allowing him to be just as he is in this moment. Being present with your child means that you let go of expectations and you appreciate who your child is right now. Marvel at this beautiful creation of God. When you are present with your child, he will sense that he is important and valuable in your eyes. He will have the sense of being the apple of your eye. This is one of the most important ways you can be sure that you are Cocooning.

Sharon walked into the family room with her child, Jake. She was tired and irritable. They had just finished lunch, typically a stressful time because Jake would rather throw his food than eat it. Jake is 5 years old and his weight is well below the growth chart. Jake began playing with his trains, crashing them together. Sharon decided to practice "being present," instead of following the urge she felt to suggest that Jake add more cars to his train. He often played aggressively and it worried her.

Sharon sat on the floor near Jake, leaned back against the couch, and closed her eyes. She took a few deep, slow breaths, making sure they filled up her abdomen and then slowly let them out through her mouth. "That feels good," she thought to herself. Then Sharon noticed how soft and comforting the couch cushion felt against her back and neck. She opened her eyes and just allowed herself to be present with Jake. She forced herself to sit quietly and let him be. She began to notice the little story Jake was creating between the train cars. She decided to observe and listen.

Now it's your turn. The following *Stop and Do: Practicing Being Present* will help you learn and practice the art of being present. Following this work, I encourage you to practice being present several times throughout the day. Do it just as you did here in the *Stop and Do*, minus the writing you did in #4. Practicing throughout the day over several days is like money in a savings account. The benefits accumulate and will help to decrease anxiety, stress, and will slow down your autonomic nervous system overall. You will find that you are calmer and your emotional reactions to situations are less intense.

**Key: Be where your feet are. Focus all of your senses and thoughts only on what is right in front of you. Your child. Not on**

## Stop and Do

**Practicing Being Present**

1). Gently stop whatever you are doing.
2). Sit quietly, close your eyes and take three slow calm breaths all the way into your abdomen and gently out through your mouth.
3). With your eyes closed and still breathing fully and gently, ask God to still your mind.
4). Next, observe and listen to the environment around you. Write down what you notice below.

What colors do you see? _____

What do you feel against your skin? _____

What sounds do you hear? _____

What smells do you notice? _____

5). If you're with your child, notice what he is doing right now. Describe what you observe in his face, gestures, voice. *(Just objective observation.)*

_____
_____
_____

6). Again, notice your breathing. Take three calming breaths all the way into your abdomen releasing the air gently through your mouth.
7). Return now to whatever needs attending to in your day in this moment.

your "to do" list or yesterday's disappointment.

**3). Refrain from asking your child questions.** I find that it is often uncomfortable for parents to sit quietly with their children, or with anyone for that matter. Talking seems to take away the anxiety. So, we usually initiate conversation by asking questions. What is he going to do next? Do you want to use this? Why is he doing that? During Cocooning, it is critical that you don't give in to this urge. Again, just be present and observe.

If you must say something, make an observation statement such as, "You have put many cars together," or "The man and the boy are on the train." Pretend you are a sports announcer giving a play-by-play of the action on the field. Don't overdo it, just make an observation statement every now and then. This may feel silly, but it is another simple means to communicate to your child that he is valuable, that what he is doing is important to you and that he is noticed by the one who loves him.

**4). Refrain from teaching.** Parents feel they always need to be teaching their child. Our interactions are comprised primarily of instructing, suggesting, labeling, informing and correcting. Here are some examples of these types of teaching statements: "How many cars do you have? One, two, three." "Let's add this piece to the track to make a mountain." "The caboose should go at the end of the train." "There are too many cars in your train. It won't make it around the curves."

During Cocooning, it is essential to refrain from such statements. Cocooning is the time when you can provide unconditional love. Remember: the purpose of Cocooning is to provide positive attachment experiences, to become more familiar with your child and to decrease trauma triggers. Instead of teaching, follow the other four Cocooning Guidelines.

**5). Let your child be your guide; join your child's**

**play.** At some point you might want to join in your child's play, or your child might invite you. Let your child be your guide to show you what to do. If your child hasn't invited you, just pick up one of the toys and do something with it that seems to fit with what he is doing. Your child might invite you to play by telling you to do something in particular or by saying something like "Play Mommy!"

Here's what this might look like: Sharon scooted a little closer to Jake and the train set he was playing with. Since Jake didn't invite her to play, she pulled a pile of wooden animals closer to her. She picked up each animal one by one and looked it over. When she set it back down, she stood it up near the train track. Jake looked a couple of times at her and then demanded, "Put the animals inside the track. We can have a zoo." Although Sharon felt a slight annoyance at being told what to do by her 5 year-old, she remembered the Cocooning Guidelines. Taking a slow deep calming breath, she began creating a zoo. Jake proceeded to give more orders, incorporating the zoo into his play. Sharon continued to follow his commands and found that she was now a part of Jake's play.

**Key: *It is the nurturing quality of your relationship with your child that helps him develop a sense of safety and the capacity for healthy relationships throughout life.***

## Helping Your Child Grow Up on the Inside

As discussed in Chapter 8, children who experience abandonment, emotional and physical deprivation, and inadequate or nonexistent nurturing so vital to the first year to two years of life, are stunted neurologically, cognitively, socially, emotionally and usually physically (the most obvious and most recognized). Orphaned children, even those adopted as early as a few months, one year, or two years, will be emotionally much younger than their chronological age.

When you first begin Cocooning, you will need to institute the ritual of "Baby Time." Baby Time is a special time between a parent (usually Mother) and the adopted child where the child will receive the nurturing they did not receive as an infant. Regardless of your child's age, during Baby Time you will hold your little one if he is comfortable with that. If he isn't, then just cuddle together. Offer a cuddly blankie and a baby bottle with either milk, juice or water; no soft drinks, Kool-Aid, etc. If you have a rocking chair, rock together, with the lights low, with lullabies playing. You might read a board book or similar baby picture book. Gaze at him, stroke his hair, talk to him like a mother of a little infant. Tell him how beautiful he is, rub his cheek gently with your finger, admire his beautiful little toes. No matter what age your child is when he comes home, start with a baby bottle.

When I first explain this to parents, they usually feel uncomfortable. They are usually worried that this will reinforce immature behavior in their child. However, just like James and his mother in Chapter 8, this is not what happens. Meeting the developmental needs of your child (according to his emotional age) will fill in the missing developmental building blocks. When these early developmental building blocks are met and satisfied, the child will begin to "grow up on the inside."

In a way, child development can be compared to the growth of a plant. When a seed is provided with the proper environmental conditions such as sunlight, water and the proper temperature, the seed will germinate, sprout, grow into a fragile seedling and eventually become a mature plant. If the fragile seedling is denied the full amount of water or sun it requires it will begin to wilt and stop growing. However, when you begin watering it again, it perks up and begins to grow again.

Remember that this helps your child to "grow up on the inside." The baby bottle will be temporary. Think about what infants need. When the early developmental needs are met, the child will begin to behave in a manner that is more consistent with, let's say, a two or three year old, and the bottle won't be needed any longer. Then you might move on to a sippie cup.

Lastly, I recommend that "Baby Time" be a limited duration and specific time of day, especially for the child who is older than a toddler. In doing this, you will be offering a "container" for Baby Time (and baby-like behavior) for the child. Good times are usually in the evening after a bath or shower and right before bed, or early in the morning. See what works for you and your family. Be flexible.

> *In family life, love is the oil that eases friction, the cement that binds closer together, and the music that brings harmony.*
> *~ Eva Burrows*

## Cocooning Activities

Here is a list of activities that are perfect for Cocooning and will help you to create a safe haven. This is not an exhaustive list, but they will give you an idea of activities appropriate for Cocooning.

**Remember:** these activities are not the time to teach your child. If your child is uncomfortable with an activity, try something else. Once you become comfortable with the Cocooning ideas presented in this book, you will more than likely come up with some of your own.

The Gotcha! Kits available from our website (NewAdoptionResources.com) has almost everything you need to get started with many of these activities:
- Baby Time
- Relaxed, playful bath time (with you inside or outside of the bathtub)
- Sharing picture books/reading
- Rocking with lullabies
- Singing/finger plays
- Playing with children's instruments
- Rub lotion all over after bath time
- Cuddling
- Gently brushing your child's hair
- Playing with early developmental toys
- Exploring nature together
- Playing in sand
- Lying in bed together
- Gentle, soft tickling
- Playing in water with simple cups

## CHAPTER 10
# Scheduling Activities Outside of Your Home

Like many adoptive parents, you may be looking into activities that will help your child make up for many of the developmental experiences she missed.

After your Gotcha! Day, your child desperately needs a safe haven. Of course, at first she won't experience you as a safe haven because she's never had one. She won't know how to take advantage of your affection, love and care. You will slowly help her learn. What your child needs most, no matter what age, is the experience of a nurturing parent who is sensitive and responsive to her needs.

During this Cocooning phase, your child needs to be close to you, and new experiences and new people must be kept to a minimum. This is the best way to help your child begin to experience you as a secure base. For this reason, the following are guidelines to help you decide how to plan activities outside the home based on the needs of your child during this Cocooning phase.

## Medical Appointments Following Gotcha Day

I strongly recommend delaying any non-serious medical procedures for at least one year. Putting a newly adopted child through medical procedures that can just as well be taken care of after one year puts your child at risk for a trauma reaction and disturbing the development of the parent-child attachment relationship.

You may think the medical procedure isn't intrusive or frightening, but it may be so to your child. If it is frightening to your child, you may not even notice. She may have learned how to keep her distressed emotions under wraps.

Attachment researchers have found that avoidantly attached children, those who seem to weather distressing events without any need for comforting, are actually very distressed as indicated by very high cortisol levels.[1] So, you can't always tell if your child is actually distressed. Remember Bowlby's three phases of loss? Initially the child protested the loss, within days she moved into a state of despair, and lastly she became psychologically detached from the loss.

A child who has lived in an orphanage or various foster homes often doesn't appear phased by distressing events. *Do not assume your child is not distressed just because she doesn't look distressed.* Assume your child experienced traumatic events in her early life. Then from there, extrapolate to any other situations that are even remotely similar in any way. Those are very likely to be

---

> **Would a Psychological Consult be Helpful for Us?**
>
> *If you check two or more boxes below, you may benefit from a psychological consult.*
>
> ☐ Sleeping or eating difficulties
>
> ☐ Child is not easily comforted
>
> ☐ Frequent temper tantrums
>
> ☐ Excessive shyness
>
> ☐ Parent has trouble bonding
>
> ☐ Recurrent feelings of disappointment on the part of parent
>
> ☐ Typical parenting strategies seem ineffective

distressful events to your child.

## Within Two Weeks of Gotcha Day: Physical Examination

If your child was adopted from an international orphanage or foster home, it is important to have a physical examination by a pediatrician knowledgeable with international adoption issues, attachment and Early Relational Trauma.

## Within First Month of Gotcha Day: Psychological Consult

A psychological consult is the next medical appointment I recommend. People often have the thought, "We don't need a psychologist!" You might feel this way. Even with all of our culture's focus on mental health and well-being it is still common for people to hesitate about seeking psychological services. Parents have told me that they felt that calling a psychologist would be an admission of failure.

I recommend this as the next medical appointment before any other medical appointments such as occupational therapy and speech therapy. I received a call from a mother who, just two weeks prior, had brought home her six year old son from another country. She was referred to our psychology practice by a pediatrician who specialized in adoption.

On the morning of the appointment, this mother called saying she needed to cancel her appointment. She went on to explain that the previous day she had taken her son for an occupational therapy assessment. According to the mother, the therapist had manipulated the child's body in order to determine the location of his trauma reactions. The mother was calling me to cancel her son's appointment because he had been "bouncing off the walls and having frequent temper tantrums" ever since the occupational therapy appointment. I asked why she scheduled the OT appointment prior to the psychological appointment. According to her, the pediatrician recommended the occupational therapy appointment prior to the psychological because he suspected Post Traumatic Stress Disorder.

This situation exemplifies how important it is that a psychological consult with the parents is scheduled prior to any non-urgent medical appointment. It is the psychologist who is trained to assess for emotional and developmental issues, to make diagnoses, and to make recommendations as the best way to help prevent, or at least minimize, the child's trauma reactions. This information would be helpful for the parents at home and to share with other professionals with whom the child must interact.

During the consult, the psychologist usually meets with both parents without the child for approximately 1 ½ -2 hours. During this time the psychologist will listen to the parents' concerns and gather background information. The psychologist typically requests any documents that provide background and history. At the end of the consult, recommendations will be offered as to whether or not a psychological evaluation is indicated. The evaluation will help to assess whether your child has any diagnosable problems such as Early Relational Trauma, depression, and/or developmental concerns.

If a psychological evaluation is recommended, it usually includes a play assessment with the child and completion of behavior rating forms by the parent. The play assessment is performed in an informal, playful and nonthreatening manner using developmentally appropriate toys. Depending on the child's age, he may be asked to complete a few specific drawings and respond to some questions as well. The interactions between you and the child will be observed as you are together in the reception area as well as following the play session. If cognitive and or developmental delays are in question, more than one session may be scheduled with your child and the psychologist in order to complete formal assessment measures.

A psychological consult performed prior to adoption as well as following your Gotcha! Day can be very helpful as well and is a great preventative measure. Of course, prior to adoption parents are only sharing written and/or video data they have received about their child.

Many of the parents we see at our office come to us once their child has begun school. This might be kindergarten, first grade or later. They often express frustration that they hadn't sought help sooner. They were looking for the signs on the list of Reactive Attachment Disorder (RAD) behaviors given to them by their adoption agency. This list includes behaviors such as a lack of remorse, lying, stealing, hoarding, aggression. Not only are these severe behaviors, but they are not usually identified prior to the start of kindergarten.

I am not a fan of the RAD Behavior Checklist for many reasons. First of all, as I stated before, the list is not founded in research. Second, the treatment that is often recommended by professionals who use this list to diagnose attachment problems usually use coercive treatment methods that are contraindicated for building secure attachment relationships and healing trauma.[4] Lastly, parents often miss many other more subtle red flag behaviors that emerge within the first year of being home with the family. Subsequently, these behaviors go undetected for years because parents thought they needed to watch for more severe behaviors found on the RAD checklist. Sadly, they don't realize that less severe behaviors can indicate Early Relational Trauma. Without proper intervention these problems are reinforced and become more ingrained in the child. Eventually the behaviors do become more severe and the parents become more and more frustrated and hopeless, causing them to finally seek treatment.

The psychologist's recommendations following the consult will be determined by the information shared by parents in the interview, the play assessment and the informal parent/child observations as well as information gleaned from documents provided by parents from the adoption process, education, or previous therapy. A psychological consult provides initial impressions and recommendations that often give parents hope and new directions.

## Benefits of a Psychological Consult

- Determines readiness to begin outside activities, such as educational and/or extracurricular activities.
- Parents: Offers direction for decreasing problematic behaviors giving parents peace of mind.
- Family: Facilitates communication and optimizes adjustment.
- Determines if child has PTSD, DID (Dissociative Identity Disorder), DDNOS (Dissociative Disorder Not Otherwise Specified), ERT (Early Relational Trauma), depression, anxiety and provide intervention recommendations.
- Screens for Sensory Integrative Disorder and, if necessary, provides referral for occupational therapy.
- Offers preliminary assessment of developmental/educational level of child and whether psychological testing is indicated.

## Guidelines for Planning Outside Activities

What your new child needs most is you and the regularity and comfort of your home. She needs to get used to you and your family. She needs a calm atmosphere. It is helpful to be home so that when your new child has a trauma or grief reaction you will not be embarrassed or stressed worrying about others' reactions. I recommend limiting activities outside of the home for the first few months even up to six months. Again, think of a newborn just coming home from the hospital. Remember that your child has Early Relational Trauma. Your job right now is to create a safe haven of regularity. A newly adopted child does not adjust well to a lot of family visits, vacations, play groups, company at home, and other similar activities. This may not be apparent at the time, but remember, your child has learned that their needs come last. It is vital that you give them the experience that their needs come first. Think about how you would feel if someone you love dearly died suddenly. How long would it take before you felt like joining your friends for a dinner out, or going to a comedy, or to a party? You must remember that this, in all likelihood, is your child's experience.

CHAPTER 11

# Using Your Gotcha! Kit

The information in this chapter will provide guidelines for using the items in the Gotcha! Kit.™ Now, you will put into action everything from the previous chapters. Guidelines will be explained for types of items; however, if you put into action the Cocooning™ Guidelines from Chapter 9, you will do well.

You may have noticed that your Gotcha! Kit doesn't contain any electronic or battery operated items. This was, as you may have guessed, purposeful. The items in your Kit may at first glance seem dull and boring compared to the items your family and friends buy for their young children. Questions such as the following may enter your mind: "Where are the Bach DVDs and the 'Teach Your Child to Read' by Age 1 CDs?" "What about the music, sounds, and lights?"

First of all, sudden lights, sounds and movement often cause anxiety for children with Early Relational Trauma by stimulating the autonomic nervous system. Secondly, a child learns a great deal by exploring and manipulating objects. This stimulates cognitive development, problem solving, and a sense of safety. Loving interaction in pleasurable activities with you will help heal attachment trauma *and* stimulate brain growth and language development.

The following is a list of the items in each of our Gotcha! Kits, in the event that you choose to assemble your kits on your own.

## Gotcha! Kit Item List

### Gotcha! Welcoming Your Child Home Basic Kit
- *Goodnight Moon* large board book
- *Pat the Bunny* book
- 1 cuddly teddy bear
- 1 soft baby
- Playskool Lullaby Glo-worm
- 1 blankie
- 1 set stacking cups
- 1 lullaby CD

### Gotcha! Welcoming Your Child Home Bath Time Kit
- 1 bathtime book
- 1 squirtie set
- 1 netted bath toy holder
- 1 set floating stacking boats
- 1 rubber duckie

### Gotcha! Welcoming Your Child Home Music Time Kit
- Little Tikes drum
- 1 small tambourine
- 1 wooden rhythm set
- 1 child's xylophone
- 1 Folk songs CD

## Cuddling and Snugglies

Your new little one has probably had very little cuddling time in her little life. As we have discussed before, this is one of primary building blocks of brain development, affect regulation development, and the development of healthy attachment styles, to name a few. Guarantee your little one gets ample cuddling time by scheduling daily Cocooning time for at least the first six months after your Gotcha! Day. Perhaps early in the morning will work for you, just after your little one arises. You might cuddle together on the couch while you read a book or listen to music. Perhaps your other children can have breakfast while you are cuddling. The two of you can just enjoy the sounds of breakfast-time in your family. Resist the temptation to put on the television during this time. If breakfast time is a challenging time for the rest of the family, plan that Dad mans the kitchen while Mom provides cuddling time.

Other "regular" cuddling times can be scheduled mid-morning and/or mid-afternoon, perhaps followed by a nap. Follow bath time or before bedtime with lullabies and a bottle. No matter what age your child is when she comes home, use a baby bottle during Cocooning at first. If this confuses you or you feel uneasy about this, reread chapter 9 where this is explained in more detail. Remember that offering a bottle will help your child to grow up on the inside. She won't need the bottle forever, she will move on to a sippie cup. To help you, I recommend thinking about infants' needs. They enjoy their bottle with Mama cuddling and singing lullabies while she gazes lovingly at her baby, in the glow of a soft light or a night light. When babies are older they want a blanket or stuffed animal to cuddle up to.

Your child may be sensitive to sounds and may seem to be disturbed or bothered by the chatter and commotion around the breakfast table. In this case, spend 15 minutes cuddling either in her room or your room. Ritualize this morning time so your little one will come to expect it and even count on it. Try as best you can to make this time occur in the same location each time. Of course, disruptions happen and changes need to be made at times.

A comfortable rocking chair provides a great place to cuddle. If you don't have one, go out and buy a glider rocker that new moms purchase especially for nursing. Make sure to purchase the little glider footstool that matches. This is one of the most relaxing chairs I've ever experienced. And, it is perfect for cuddling with your little one. You might prefer an overstuffed chair or a couch.

Be sure to offer a soft baby blanket with the satin edging and a fluffy stuffed animal for your little one.

A wonderful book with lots of ideas for lullabies, finger plays, and other Cocooning activities is Becky A. Bailey's book, *I Love You Rituals*.

## Reading a Picture Book with Your Child

Reading helps to create a special bond between parent and child. Reading also stimulates brain growth.

Choose books with colors, textures, and characters. Even if you child is a toddler, read picture books with large colorful pictures on every page. You might even want to begin with board books. Choose books that are for very young children like *Goodnight Moon*, by Margaret Wise Brown and *Jamberry*, by Bruce Degan. When reading a picture book with your child, take time to look at the pictures. Cuddling is also wonderful when you read picture books together. Wait to turn the page when your child seems satiated with commenting on the colors, objects, people, animals, or just looking at the pictures. Read gently, slowly; don't rush on to the next page. Savor each page with your child, taking in the beauty of the illustrations as well as the words. Allow yourself to feel this experience you are sharing with your child.

Remember the guideline for Cocooning, "Let your child be

your guide; join your child's play." If your child wants to turn the page, let him. If he wants to point, "read," or talk let him. If he wants to crawl away before the book is finished, let him, saying something like, "You want to do something else now," or "I don't think you want to read anymore right now." If you have other children, let them join in. Snuggle up together on the couch, bed or even the floor with a soft blanket and pillows.

Remember the Cocooning guideline, "Refrain from teaching." Just enjoy the book with your child. Do not ask him to repeat words or point to words you say. Do not ask him to point to parts of the illustration you name. However, you may point to parts of the illustration as you talk about it. Your child will naturally join in the "game" and point, repeat, and ask questions. He may not join in the first time you read the book or the tenth. Be patient with yourself, with your child and with the developmental process. All of this is probably a very novel experience for your child.

## Playing with Early Developmental Toys

All of these toys in your Kit have been chosen because of their developmental aspects, versatility, durability, attractiveness, and ease with which one can limit sensory stimulation. Remember that your Gotcha! Kit is not intended to be educational. Yes, it will help brain development, but the purpose of the Kit is to help your child develop a secure attachment with you and to begin to heal her Early Relational Trauma. Your sensitivity and responsiveness and the pleasurable, relaxed encounters will make this possible.

Resist the pressure from those around you, family, friends and professionals who feel you need to always be teaching your child and to be "working" with your child to bring them up to where they should be for their chronological age. I encourage you to resist. With insecure attachments parents often interact with their children in a

## Using Your Gotcha! Kit

## Stop and Do

**Sending Away the "Shoulds"**
1). Gently stop yourself.
2). Stop now, sit quietly, close your eyes and take three slow calm breaths all the way into your abdomen and gently through your mouth.
3). With your eyes closed and still breathing fully and gently, ask God to put a loving, gentle reminder in your thoughts.
4). When you have the words, write them down.
5). During Cocooning time, when negative, critical thoughts enter your mind, stop, take a few deep, gentle breaths and say your phrase. Say it to yourself, remembering to breathe gently, until you feel relaxed and fully present in the moment.

functional way as opposed to parents of securely attached children who tend to interact with their children in authentic, intimate ways. What's the difference you might ask?

Tommy, a four year old boy who was 13 months old on their Gotcha! Day, was feeling scared and anxious about because his mother had just left for an overnight trip. Unable to express these emotions, he became distractible and overactive. Kneeling down beside his son, his father stated, "You have some big feelings inside." Tommy put his hand on dad's knee and leaned against him. "I wonder if you might be having some feelings about Mommy going away." Tommy said meekly, "She won't come back." Dad then proceeded to reassure Tommy that his mother would be returning, showing him the days on the calendar, and put a framed photo of Mother in view of Tommy. He also stayed closer to Tommy and spent time playing and reading with him frequently while Mother was away.

It is important to resist the temptation to give in to the "shoulds." When you start thinking "I should be doing ____," or "What would my mother think if she saw me doing this?" that is when you need to help yourself to remember the purpose of Cocooning, to heal your child's Early Relational Trauma, build a secure attachment with your child, and to fill in developmental building blocks in order to facilitate emotional, cognitive, and social maturation. Take a look at *Stop and Do: Sending Away the "Shoulds"* on the following page to use whenever you get a case of the "shoulds."

## Bath Time

Bath time can be a pleasurable, relaxing time for you and your child. Older infants and toddlers especially love being in and playing with water. To ensure that you won't get frustrated with the amount of time it might take, allow yourself a good half an hour for the bath. We have a Gotcha! Kit specifically for bath time. Use bubbles only if your child is comfortable with them.

Fill the bath with several inches of warm water. Choose a few of the toys to put in the water. You can let your child choose saying, "Choose three toys," counting as he chooses. If this creates a struggle, just put some toys in as you run the bath. If your child wants all the toys, put all the toys in the bath.

Sit on the floor or on a short stool beside the bathtub. Remember to be aware of your breathing, slowing it down and breathing deeply and gently. You can use this time to let go of stress and relax. Follow your child's lead. Watch your child's play. Narrate your child's play to let him know that you are present with him and that what he is doing is important to you. Don't overdo it. Remember, it's okay to sit quietly fiddling in the water with a toy. Join in with your child's play if he seems to enjoy that. If you have bubbles, put bubbles on your baby's face like a beard. Have a child's bath mirror on the side of the tub and encourage your child to look at himself. Laugh, sing, have fun.

## Music

Music can be employed at different times of the day. Quiet, soothing music for times when you need to slow down your child, help your child to calm his nervous system, or to encourage sleep. Choose music that is high quality music for children as well as other music such as classical, cultural, and folk. For quiet time choose time tested lullabies such as those included in the Gotcha! Kit. Once you find a CD that your child responds positively to, return to it. There is no need to have a multitude of CDs. One to three CDs is enough. Familiarity will add to your child's comfort and will create a positive association with the music.

The other use for music is time for cuddling together while you sing, dance, and/or engage in finger plays together. Be gentle, sit with your child in your arms or on your lap, or if he is more comfortable on the floor facing you. This is a great way to have some eye contact that is natural and enjoyable. Remember to let go of your expectations and be present in the moment. Help your child learn the finger play or song, but if he is resistant to it, follow along with what he is comfortable doing. Dance or move around the room to the music, hold colorful scarves in the air, or play along with small instruments such as bells, tambourine, or rhythm sticks.

Stay with this until your child seems to become distracted or disinterested, even if it's only a few minutes. You want this to be a pleasurable experience. Make comments such as, "I love singing with you."

Now that we have gone over some general categories of Cocooning activities and applying the guidelines to each, you are armed with skills that can be generalized to most of your interactions with your child. Remember, though, that the Cocooning Guidelines are for Cocooning times. It is important to remember that your child also needs clear limits and structure. This will help your child feel safe. When you are setting limits, remember to use developmentally appropriate limits with your child's emotional age in mind, not his chronological age. As you do this, along with Cocooning, your child will grow up on the inside.

The goal of Cocooning is emotional development; specifically, to help your child grow up on the inside. As you meet these early developmental and attachment needs, and your child begins to heal from their trauma wounds, your child will grow from the first stage of development into the next stage of separation/individuation. Psychologists like to say that in the first year of life, parents should be sensitive and responsive to the infant's needs in a "good enough" way. After the first year of life, children need to begin to experience delay of gratification, disappointment and frustration in small measure. They need to learn to play on their own and with other children. They need to learn that you have other tasks and interests that are also important, and which sometimes take priority.

Often times, parents with whom I have worked believe they need to keep Cocooning indefinitely. This is not healthy for the child or the parents or the family as a whole. Yes, certainly continue Cocooning, but time spent Cocooning will decrease as independent play or play with others increases. It will decrease while you take care of other responsibilities, establish healthy boundaries, and responsibilities. I encourage all families to continue reading aloud, incorporating classics, as a family well into the middle school ages or beyond. Continue spending quality time together; this is essential for maneuvering through the complex period of adolescence.

To help you recognize when your child is "growing up on the

inside" and moving up the developmental spectrum, I recommend getting a basic book on normal ages and stages of child development such as *Ages and Stages: A Parent's Guide to Normal Childhood Development* by Charles E. Schaefer and Theresa Foy DiGeronimo. For links to this and other books and resources, please visit our website, NewAdoptionResources.com.

# Notes

### Chapter 2: The "Mission of Adopting an Orphaned Child
1). Statistics. Retrieved February 5, 2011,
   from http://thirdworldorphans.org
2). Statistics. Retrieved February 5, 2011,
   from http://hopefororphansoftheworld.org/default.aspx?id=30
3). Statistics. Retrieved February 5, 2011,
   from http://www.worldorphanproject/statistics.html
4). Statistics. Retrieved February 5, 2011,
   from http://harvestministry.org/orphan-stats
5). Statistics. Retrieved February 5, 2011,
   from http://savingorphansforjesus2010.blogspot.com/2010/05/orphan-statistics-why-we-are-adopting.html
6). Thomas, N. L. (2005) *When love is not enough: a guide to parenting children with RAD-Reactive Attachment Disorder*, Families By Design, Glenwood Springs, CO; Gregory C. Keck, G. C. & Kupecky, R. (2009) (Ed.) L.G. Mansfield. *Adopting the hurt child: Revised and updated: Hope for families with special-needs kids*, NavPress Publishing Co., Colorado Springs, CO;

Cline, F. & Fay, J. (1990) *Parenting with love and logic: Teaching children responsibility*, Pinon Press, Colorado Springs, CO.
7). Chaffin, M., Hanson, R., Saunders, B. E., Nichols, T., Barnett, D., Zeanah, C. Berliner, L., Egeland, B., Newman, E., Lyon, T., Letourneau, E., Miller-Perrin, C. (2006). Report of the APSAC task force on attachment therapy, Reactive Attachment Disorder, and attachment problems. *Child Maltreatment*, 11, 76-89.
8). Schore, A.N. (2001). The effects of early relational trauma on right brain development, affect regulation, and infant mental health. In *Infant Mental Health Journal*, ed. A.N. Schore, Vol. 22, 201-269.
9). DSouza, R.(2002). Do patients expect psychiatrists to be interested in spiritual issues? *Australas Psychiatry*, 10, 44-47; Tepper L., Rogers, S.A., Coleman E. M., eta al. (2001). The prevalence of religious coping among persons with persistent mental illness. *Psychiatric Services*, 52, 660-665; Koenig, H.G. (2008). Religion and Mental health: What should psychiatrists do? *Psychiatric Bulletin*, 32, 201-203.

## Chapter 3: The First Missing Piece: Nurturing

1). Sroufe, L. A. (2005). Attachment and development: A prospective, longitudinal study from birth to adulthood, *Attachment and Human Development*, 7, 349-367.
2). Harlow, H. F. (1958). The nature of love. *American Psychologist*, 13, 673-685.
3). Ibid.
4). Bowlby J. (1969). *Attachment. Attachment and Loss*: Vol. 1. Loss. New York: Basic Books.
5). Bell, S. M,, & Ainsworth, M. D. S. (1972). Infant crying and maternal responsiveness. *Child Development*, 43, 1171-1190; Sroufe, L. A. (2005). Attachment and development: A prospective, longitudinal study from birth to adulthood, *Attachment and Human Development*, 7, 349-367.
6). Ibid.
7). Winnicott, D. (1953). Transitional objects and transitional phenomena, *International Journal of Psychoanalysis*, 34, 89-97.
8). Bell, S. M,, & Ainsworth, M. D. S. (1972). Infant crying and maternal responsiveness. *Child Development*, 43, 1171-1190; Sroufe, L. A. (2005).

Attachment and development: A prospective, longitudinal study from birth to adulthood, *Attachment and Human Development*, 7, 349-367.
9). Schore, A.N. (2001). The effects of early relational trauma on right brain development, affect regulation, and infant mental health. In *Infant Mental Health Journal*, ed. A.N. Schore, Vol. 22, 201-269.

## Chapter 4: The Second Missing Piece: Early Relational Trauma

1). Bowlby, J. (1969). Attachment and loss, vol. 1: Attachment. London: Pimlico.
2). Crittenden, P.M. & Ainsworth M.D.S. (1989). Child maltreatment and attachment theory. In D. Cicchetti and V. Carlson (Eds.), *Handbook of child maltreatment*, (pp. 432-463). New York: Cambridge University Press.; Erickson, M. F., Egeland, B., & Pianta, R. (1989). The effects of maltreatment on the development of young children. In D. Cicchetti and V. Carlson (Eds.), Child Maltreatment: Theory and Research on the Causes and Consequences of Child Abuse and Neglect (pp. 647-684), Cambridge University Press; Schore, A.N. (2001). The effects of early relational trauma on right brain development, affect regulation, and infant mental health. In *Infant Mental Health Journal*, ed. A.N. Schore, Vol. 22, 201-269.
3). Schore, A.N. (2001). The effects of early relational trauma on right brain development, affect regulation, and infant mental health. In *Infant Mental Health Journal*, ed. A.N. Schore, Vol. 22, 201-269.
4). Liotti, G. (1992). Disorganized/disoriented attachment in the etiology of the dissociative disorders. In *Dissociation*, 4:196-204.
5). Perry - Adaptive Response to Threat.
6). Liotti, G. (1992). Disorganized/disoriented attachment in the etiology of the dissociative disorders. In *Dissociation*. 4:196-204; Carlson, E., Yates, T., & Sroufe, L.A. (2009). Development of dissociation and development of the self. In P. Dell, J. O'Neil, & E. Somer (Eds.), *Dissociation and dissociative disorders*. New York: Routledge.
7). Ibid.
8). Robertson, J. & Bowlby, J. (1952), Responses of young children to separation from their mothers. *Courrier of the International Children's Centre*, Paris, II, 131-140.

9). Perry, B., Pollard, R., Blakley, T., Baker, W., & Vigilante, D. (1995). Childhood trauma, the neurobiology of adaptation, and "use-dependent" development of the brain: How ..states "become.. traits". *Infant Mental Health Journal*, 16, 271-291.

## Chapter 5: The Third Missing Piece: Parenting is Hard!
1). Thomas, A. & Chess, S. (1989). *Temperament in clinical practice*. The Guilford Press, New York, NY.
2). Ibid.
3). Kurcinka, M. S. (2006). *Raising your spirited child: a guide for parents whose child is more intense, sensitive, perceptive, persistent, and energetic*. HarperCollins Publishers, New York, NY.

## Chapter 6: The Fourth Missing Piece: You
1). Bowlby J. (1969). *Attachment. Attachment and Loss*: Vol. 1. Loss. New York: Basic Books.

## Chapter 7: The Fifth Missing Piece: God
1). DSouza, R.(2002). Do patients expect psychiatrists to be interested in spiritual issues? *Australas Psychiatry*, 10, 44-47; Tepper L., Rogers, S.A., Coleman E. M., eta al. (2001). The prevalence of religious coping among persons with persistent mental illness. *Psychiatric Services*, 52, 660-665; Koenig, H.G. (2008). Religion and Mental health: What should psychiatrists do? *Psychiatric Bulletin*, 32, 201-203.
2). Vitz, P. C., (2000). Faith of the fatherless: The psychology of atheism. Spence Publishing Co. Dallas, TX.

## Chapter 8: Cocooning Part 1: What & Why
1). Mahler, M. S., Pine, F. & Bergman, A. (1975). The psychological birth of the human infant: symbiosis and individuation. Basic Books, New York, NY.
2). Sroufe, L. A. (2005). Attachment and development: A prospective, longitudinal study from birth to adulthood, *Attachment and Human Development*. 7, 349-367.
3). Thomas, A. & Chess, S. (1989). Temperament in clinical practice. The

Guilford Press, New York, NY.

## Chapter 9: Cocooning Part 2: How?
1). Bell, S. M., & Ainsworth, M. D. S. (1972). Infant crying and maternal responsiveness. *Child Development*, 43, 1171-1190.
2). Bowlby J. (1969). *Attachment. Attachment and Loss*: Vol. 1. Loss. New York: Basic Books.
3). June 5, 2011. found in http://dictionary.reference.com/browse/ritual

## Chapter 10: Scheduling Activities Outside of Your Home
1). Hertsgaard, L., Gunnar, M., Erickson, M., & Nachmias, M. (1995). Adreno-cortical responses to the Strange Situation in infants with disorganised/disoriented attachment relationships. *Child Development*, 66, 1100---1106.
2). Chaffin, M., Hanson, R., Saunders, B. E., Nichols, T., Barnett, D., Zeanah, C. Berliner, L., Egeland, B., Newman, E., Lyon, T., Letourneau, E., Miller-Perrin, C. (2006). Report of the APSAC task force on attachment therapy, Reactive Attachment Disorder, and attachment problems. *Child Maltreatment*, 11, 76-89.

## Chapter 11: Using Your Gotcha! Kit
1). Bailey, B. A. (2000). *I Love You Rituals*. HarperCollins Publishers Inc., New York, NY.
2). Brown, M. W. (2005) *Goodnight Moon*.
3). Degan, B. (2000). *Jamberry*. HarperCollins Publishers Inc., New York, NY.
4). Schaefer, C. E. & DiGeronimo, T. F.(2000). *Ages and Stages: A Parent's Guide to Normal Childhood Developmental*. John Wiley & Sons, Inc. New York, NY.

# About the Author

At the writing of this book, Patti M. Zordich, Ph.D. is a licensed psychologist in Cary, North Carolina. She is Director of Triangle Psychological Services, a psychology group with a mission to integrate psychology and faith, which she founded in 2008. Dr. Zordich specializes in helping families with attachment and Early Relational Trauma issues. She uses play therapy, art therapy, sandplay therapy, and talk therapy with children and parent-relationship therapy with their parents. As a consultant she provides trainings for groups and individuals on therapeutic interventions for children and families with Early Relational Trauma. She also enjoys providing therapy for adults suffering from PTSD, depression and anxiety as well as providing marriage counseling.

In one way or another, Dr. Zordich has been immersed in attachment and childhood trauma since 1990. The first six years included doctoral studies and a graduate assistantship on a research project at the University of Pittsburgh (her hometown) grounded in attachment and developmental research. During the next ten years, she provided psychological services to children and families in the foster care system and foster parents including play therapy, art therapy, sandtray therapy and family therapy. During this time she also designed and implemented a forensic psychological assessment to assess the quality of parent-child relationship using attachment research and theory, often testifying in family court as an expert witness.

Dr. Zordich grew up in Pittsburgh and is the youngest of seven children. She lived there until relocating to North Carolina with her husband and their son in 2006. She currently resides with her husband and son and their dog, Roscoe, in North Carolina.

Made in the USA
Middletown, DE
14 March 2018